STEWART COWLEY

SMALL GARDENS
and
PATIOS

Marshall Cavendish

Published by Marshall Cavendish Books Limited
58 Old Compton Street
London W1V 5PA

© Marshall Cavendish Limited 1986

Printed and bound in Hong Kong by
Dai Nippon Printing Company

First printing 1976
This printing 1986

ISBN 0 85685 158 2

Introduction

A small garden is a garden for today. The high cost of building land and the ever-increasing pace of life has brought it into its own, demanding a reappraisal of its special characteristics.

Small Gardens and Patios will open up new vistas to the owner of a small garden – showing him how to plan it, incorporating features such as rock gardens and trellis-work to their best advantage. Whether you live in town or country the colourful pictures and illustrations will inspire you to rediscover your garden's potential. Find out how to make the most of a garden enclosed by walls – or how to create an effect of 'ordered chaos' in an old cottage garden.

Flat-dwellers have not been forgotten. Unconventional growing areas – a back yard, basement, balcony or roof garden – can be filled with beautiful blooms to brighten the view on the dullest day.

Learn how to make window boxes and hanging baskets – how to enliven a patio and care for container plants. Discover that vegetables, fruit and herbs can be grown in tiny spaces, both for ornamental and culinary purposes.

All types of small garden are included here – so whether it is modern or traditional, shaded or sunny, at ground or roof level – before you finish reading you will be inspired to start planning next season's display in your own small garden.

Left: *A charming small garden that incorporates many features that can be successfully utilized in a limited area. The design emphasizes the value of wall and overhead growing space by including a number of attractive wall plants, climbers and hanging baskets.*

Overleaf: *This small garden is laid out in a formal manner. The beds, which are separated by old brick paths, are mainly filled with herbs. Annuals, low-growing perennials and flowering sub-shrubs could have been planted instead to create a bright array of colour.*

Contents

A garden for today

In the years previous to World War I, it was fashionable for the middle and upper classes to have large gardens, which increased in size in relation to an owner's social status. Even many of the poor people, who lived in houses with little more than a backyard, or in tenements with no open space attached at all, worked allotments, where they grew vegetables and fruit and sometimes flowers. These allotments, with a standard area of 252 sq m (300 sq yd), were often considerably larger than many present-day gardens.

Small gardens today

With the passage of time there have been great changes in our concepts of gardening and gardens. That many people today possess small gardens is due to a number of factors. Probably the most significant of these is the scarcity and the excessively high cost of building land, particularly during the past ten years or so. This has had the effect of both forcing newly erected houses to be built on small plots, and of inducing persons with large gardens to reduce their own commitment considerably, sometimes by selling parcels of ground for building purposes.

Another cause that has contributed very considerably to the reduction in the size of gardens, has been the scarcity of skilled gardening labour and the higher wages now demanded by the few gardeners remaining. With the increasing rate of inflation, it has become very difficult for many people to maintain large areas of garden.

Even those who have still retained the full space around their residence have cut back on the upkeep by, for example, allowing a substantial proportion of it to turn into a wild garden or by using labour-saving ground cover plants. Another factor that might have brought about, to some extent, the smaller gardens of today is the increased cost of the trees, shrubs and other plants.

In addition small gardens are more in keeping with the mode of living today when compared with the more leisurely times of our forbears. Most people have full-time occupations which leave them only weekends to garden, and they are unable to give the exacting attention that a large garden calls for, if it is not rapidly to become a wilderness. Gardening has also to compete for available time with other leisure activities or do-it-yourself tasks in the home.

Allotments

With the increased price of vegetable produce there is a renewed interest in allotments (particularly from those living in towns who have little or no gardening space around their homes),

Below: *A well-filled colourful small garden, laid out informally, which would provide an attractive outlook from an older house in a built-up area.*

as they enable people to grow their own vegetables, fruit and flowers. Although existing letting conditions do not yet permit it, it is conceivable that the allotment may in future provide an opportunity to those who live in built-up areas to develop the land along the lines that exist in some countries on the continent. The continental allotment, usually situated on the outskirts of a town, provides a family pleasure ground with its weekend chalet, lawns, flowers and produce.

Size

One of the greatest difficulties that confronts anybody who commences to discuss this subject is to define what is a small garden. It is recorded that the average size of the $14\frac{1}{2}$ million gardens in Britain is 186 sq m (2000 sq ft) which is, say, 15m (50ft) x 12m (40ft). Needless to say, as this is a mean size, there must be a considerable number smaller than this. The size of the gardens of many fairly large, newly-built houses in urban areas rarely exceeds a width of 18m (60ft) across and 12m (40ft) in length. These dimensions will be regarded as the very maximum that can be said to fall into the small garden category. Many people will find that their own garden is very much smaller, but from the planting and planning point of view, the problems are mainly common.

Below: *Many suburban front gardens today are used for car parking. In this one, to compensate for the loss of flower beds and lawn at ground level, advantage has been taken of the bare walls by planting climbers against them to create interest at eye-level.*

Below: *For those who have little room to grow anything, a window box is one way of creating a 'small space garden'.*

Bottom: *Cottage gardens today are often small. Here, full use has been made of vertical space, container plants and a narrow flower bed.*

Problems and planning

Small gardens, whether in town or country, all have handicaps that have to be overcome. Perhaps the most prominent of these is securing privacy, because areas of small dimensions are often overlooked. Screening must be introduced in such a way that it does not close in the already rather congested area, or throw a complete shadow over the whole garden, or, perhaps worse, that of the neighbour's. In built-up areas, among old houses, concealing a next-door window might contravene the old laws regarding ancient lights.

One of the problems of the larger of the small gardens is that they are usually rectangular in shape and enclosed by high fences (possibly a virtue in a courtyard or patio, where formality must rule). In these it is usually more pleasing to create informality, to give a sense of fluidity, by means of curved lawns and variations in shape and height of the shrubs and other plants included.

Planning your garden is most important. By using certain devices you can 'correct' a badly-shaped garden – or by incorporating features such as a rock garden, trellis-work or a herb border you can create interest in an otherwise dull layout.

Small town and cottage gardens each have special problems of their own and are dealt with separately in this book. In the case of the former you may have to decide whether to pave the area or lay a lawn, while for a cottage garden a knowledge of which plants to grow is necessary if you wish to achieve an effect of 'ordered chaos'.

Patios and roof gardens have become increasingly popular in recent years and enable you to make full use of containers, in which a variety of plants can be grown. Care must be taken when building or altering either of the above, as local bye-laws or a landlord's agreement may forbid certain structural alterations. Find out if these apply to your dwelling before making plans.

At ground level too the same advice applies. For example, you will need the permission of your local authority for the erection of a shed or greenhouse (whose dimensions exceed a statutory minimum size) and sometimes for new external walls. Some trees have roots that undermine foundations, so care should be taken to see that nothing is planted which is likely to do damage to your own house and, even more important, that of your neighbour who might sue you for damages.

Small space gardens

Although gardens are smaller nowadays, this does not deter the inherent desire in many to grow something – possibly a primitive instinct inherited from the past, when survival was the predominant motivating force. This wish to grow something has been shown, over the last few years, by the increasing numbers of people buying houseplants.

If you do not own a ground level or roof garden, but still wish to grow something outside then consider other alternatives. Make full use of all available growing space which is accessible from your living area, whether it is a backyard, basement, balcony or window box. This book will show you how to grow plants, vegetables, fruit and herbs in the smallest of areas, which besides being a satisfying pastime is one that brings economic as well as aesthetic rewards.

Your own garden

No matter what is the size of your gardening space, its condition or its environment, it can be made attractive and productive. Moreover, by careful planning and planting it can be made labour-saving to the extent that it should need no more than two hours' work per week, for the largest area considered in this book, to keep it in perfect condition.

Lists are given, in the following pages, of various sorts of plants that are most suited to the different kinds of gardens discussed. Advice is also given to help you plan the development of your garden, as charming little plants that captivate the hearts of all when they are young can become overwhelming giants within a few years.

With regard to obtaining advice on plants and planting, you will usually find your local garden centre very helpful. Also, you might find it useful, as well as pleasurable, to join a horticultural society, if there is one in your neighbourhood.

Finally, owners of small gardens today can draw inspiration from the large gardens of a past age, whose owners added to their charm and serenity by creating small rose, tulip, iris, paeony, herb, Elizabethan knot gardens and so on, all surrounded by smaller hedges, within their own boundaries. Two excellent examples of this type of garden, both of which are often open to the public, are Sissinghurst Castle and Hidcote Manor.

Above: *These newly-completed town houses only need a garden enthusiast to give each one an individual character. Climbers could be grown to scale the bare walls, colourful bulbs and annuals in containers could brighten a balcony, or be planted in window boxes. Shrubs and other plants in tubs could be placed around the front porch to create a pleasing welcome.*

Left: *Owners of small gardens should visit the beautiful large gardens of stately homes, palaces and castles to see tiny areas, enclosed by hedges, devoted to various types of plants. The gardens of Sissinghurst Castle, shown here, are just one example.*

The small garden

Below: *In this well-designed small garden gently flowing lines of shrubs, grass, rock and water form interesting shades and clumps of colour.*

Opposite page, left: *The garden of a stone house in the Cotswolds with a formal pool, which is neatly bordered by slabs of roughly-hewn stone.*

Opposite page, right: *A two-year-old garden of an urban semi-detached house which has been artistically planned in a modern style. The well-kept lawn is set off by the neat borders and a curving path.*

Whether you decide to lay out your garden in a formal manner or in the style of a cottage garden, a degree of planning will be necessary to achieve the best results. This chapter explains how to plan your garden and suggests features for it which require only the minimum of space, besides providing focal points.

Planning your garden

If your garden is brand new, or if you wish to redesign it, you may find it valuable to draw a plan of your site before you start planning or positioning any features.

To do this you need a large piece of either centimetre or inch graph paper.

The site and any features must be drawn on this to scale. A convenient scale for this purpose is 1:100, which is given by a scale of 1 centimetre to 1 metre or $\frac{1}{8}$ inch to 1 foot.

Measure up the house and draw it to scale on the squared paper (ABCD). It is now necessary to draw in the boundary fence. This is done by selecting two points on the back boundary, E and F. Then measure with a tape the distances AE and BE. Pinpoint E on the plan by setting a pair of compasses to the distance AE to the scale, placing the compass point in the squared paper at A, and describing an arc. Draw another with the compasses set at the distance BE and the point at B. The place at which they intersect

represents the point E on the fence. Repeat this process to find point F.

Join the points E and F and extend the line both ways. Do this again to mark the positions G and H, K and L and I and J on the right hand, left hand and front boundaries respectively. Then extend each of the straight lines through them until they meet. The resulting figure MNOP represents the outline of the site drawn to scale. Next mark the direction of North.

It is now important to look at the site and decide which existing features should remain. It might be a tree, Q on the plan. It is necessary to position this accurately. This is done by measuring its distance with a tape from two adjacent corners (A and B) of the house.

The compass point is then put into A on the plan and set to a distance representing the length AQ on the scale and an arc is described. This is repeated from point B using the distance BQ scaled down as the radius. The point where the two arcs cross marks the position of the tree Q. Any other features are similarly positioned using the sides of the house as base lines.

Garden features

However small your garden, it should have at least one main feature, or focal point. It may be an ornamental pool, a paved terrace bordered by beautiful rose beds, a sundial or a rock garden.

When you have decided on these features, position them carefully on your plan. Do not forget the compass direction of the facing aspect, the wind, soil or other factors which must be taken into consideration.

Try to set off the features naturally with contrasting elements. For example, a pool could be set off by a lawn and a lawn by a border of shrubs and herbaceous plants. If the pool is of an informal shape it could be backed with a carefully-built bank of rocks and stones. There are infinite variations and possibilities. Let the main features show up as focal points in the garden, and then let the lawns and borders provide a neat, simple foil for them, always remembering that you want to keep maintenance work in the garden to a

minimum. Keep the lawn as large as is practicable. Besides being much less work to keep tidy than borders, a large lawn, in proportion to the rest of the garden, will make the latter appear much larger than it really is. If you wish to have an undulating lawn, give careful attention to the drainage of the depressions, or you may have trouble later.

Let at least one of your features be as far away from the house as possible, so that in attracting the eye to it in the distance you will be making full use of the length of your garden. Do not forget the value of vistas, or framed views, when designing and planting. A white-painted seat or a bed of scarlet floribunda roses are good distant eye-catchers. By planting a shrub border with a break in it, you could create a framed view just as a painter might do.

Avoid the temptation to include more items than would be practical — remember that a garden overcrowded with features is probably less satisfying and more difficult to maintain than one of quiet simplicity. Too many features just crowd the garden and make unnecessary work.

The illustration opposite shows one way in which you could design your own small garden once you have made a basic plan. A wide variety of plants and shrubs have been included and a trellis, a rock garden, rose beds and a kitchen garden are features that have been incorporated without overcrowding the space available. The illustration below

Above: *A sundial, surrounded by paving and appropriate plants, can form a centre-piece in a small garden.*

Below: *A triangular site packed with well-proportioned features. A circular lawn can be particularly valuable in a very small plot because it gives a sense of spaciousness.*

Left: *A typical design for a small garden showing compactness and a wide variety of plants and shrubs. This illustrated plan is for a semi-detached plot. The ground slopes about 1m (3ft) from the end of the back garden down to the front. This was taken into consideration in planning the rock out-crops, which form a rockery on the right; the lower rock bed on the left; the steps from the rear lawn to the terrace, and the step from the path to the front door down to the lawn. The well-kept lawn is outlined by the gentle curves of the flower beds, giving an informal effect.*

Climbers have been planted to train over the 1.5m (5ft) high square mesh trellis across the back of the border, at the end of the lawn, to screen the kitchen garden. The entrance to the latter is partially hidden by the bed of roses, which also forms a distant focal point. Apart from providing room for fruit trees the kitchen garden could also be the site for a tool shed, or possibly a greenhouse, depending on requirements and space. A compost heap might also be placed here. The birdbath, set on a square of paving stones, between which alpines could be grown, forms a secondary focal point in this garden. The continuous movement of thirsty birds creates interest all through the year. The wall retaining the higher level of the rose beds and lawn from the rear terrace is an important feature, as it is always in full view of the house. Give much thought to the selection of the material with which you build this wall. It should provide a pleasing foil for the plants and blend effectively with the paving. Remember that any paving laid must slope down slightly away from the house, so that rain does not lie against the brickwork and perhaps soak down to the foundations. The main borders have been planted with flowering and evergreen shrubs, interspersed with hardy herbaceous perennials. Tall shrubs give privacy to the terrace from the left side and to the garden on the right boundary where they are intermixed with conifers. In the front garden the colourful flowers in the front and side beds leave the centre of the lawn open, while the tree in the corner acts as a focal point to divert the eye from a car parked in the drive, or from passing traffic in the road.

House

Area

Above: *A lawn takes less time to maintain than borders. As long as it is in proportion to the size of the garden, it should be made as large as possible .When a lawn is bordered by curved beds or paths it assumes an informal appearance.*

Top right: *The grass on a newly-sown lawn should be only clipped over lightly with hand shears. Alternatively a mower can be used with the blades set high, when the grass is about 8cm (3in) high.*

Bottom right: *Most annual weeds can be removed by mowing, but perennial weeds, which appear in the sward, should be removed by hand. Particular attention should be given to tufts of coarse, undesirable grasses, such as the varieties 'Yorkshire Fog' or 'Creeping Soft Grass', which cannot be killed by hormone weed killers.*

shows how a central round lawn softens the angularity of an awkwardly-shaped garden. Both plans indicate principles to assist you in designing your own garden. The rest of the chapter will explain how to choose and care for the main features in your garden and how to use them to their best advantage.

The lawn

Whether you design the lawn on formal or informal lines, make any curves gentle ones to render the task of mowing easier. Sharp curves are much more difficult to mow round. For the same reason, any beds in the lawn should be roughly fish-shaped, broad in the centre, tapering to a point at each end, rather than circular, oval or rectangular.

To make a good lawn the site should be dug, removing all weeds, and grass fertilizer incorporated in the top soil, preferably in late summer. It should then be raked level and allowed to stand for a few weeks. All coarse grass should then be dug out and weeds killed by watering with a proprietary mixture of paraquat and diquat to produce a clean seed bed. After this, the

surface should be raked to a fine tilth, preferably with a wooden rake, removing stones.

Unless you have access to a turf specialist, you should use grass seed, because good turf is a rare commodity. The best time to sow is late summer (or alternatively in spring, if necessary). About 56gms (2oz) per square metre of seed should be evenly distributed, covered with soil by raking and rolled in lightly. The first mowing should be done with the mower bottom blade set high, when the grass is 7.5cm (3in) high.

Grass is often badly neglected. It should be kept free of weeds, fertilized in the autumn, spring and through summer, with a proprietary fertilizer, and regularly watered, particularly during drought as it is important that the grass is never allowed to brown.

Beds and borders

It will save much trouble later, if, before any work is done on the actual layout of a new garden, the whole area is first of all forked clear of all weeds and rubbish. As far as the planting is concerned, as many shrubs, roses and

herbaceous plants should be included as possible. Not only does this provide a more natural and lasting effect, but in the long run it saves labour and expense.

The quality of your soil will determine your choice of plants. Find out about the soil in your garden – its acidity or alkalinity – so that you will know what type of fertilizer and how much humus to add to your soil.

This will give you a guide as to which plants you will be able to grow.

Keeping beds free of weeds, preferably by regular hoeing, is important. Mulch by spreading a 5cm (2in) layer of rotted farmyard manure, garden compost or peat over the surface of the moist soil in late spring. This will retain moisture. Water during dry spells and dress the soil each spring with general fertilizer for shrubs and herbaceous plants and rose fertilizer for roses. Lift, divide and replant herbaceous perennials every three to four years.

Additional colour may, if required, be provided by summer-flowering annuals and biennials, but hardy herbaceous perennials, shrubs and trees should form a permanent backbone to your scheme. Sometimes the various terms applied to plants confuse beginners. Garden plants fall broadly into three categories:—

(1) Annuals – flower, go to seed and die in the same year as their seeds are sown.

(2) Biennials – flower, seed and then die the year after they are sown.

(3) Perennials – are plants that live for three or more years and flower in their second and subsequent years.

Two other main divisions for plants are:—

(a) Softwood plants – include annuals,

Above: *A well-planned herbaceous border, giving massed colour during the summer, is set off by a well-kept lawn. Pot plants and a stone plinth have been introduced to achieve a gradual change from the informal atmosphere of the garden to the formal one of the house.*

Left: *Curving paths can create an element of surprise, even in a small garden. The large pebbles between the concrete slabs of this path give it an informal, natural look.*

biennials and herbaceous plants, which themselves die back in autumn and shoot again the following spring.

(b) Hardwood plants – are trees and shrubs.

Bulb, corm and rhizome plants are softwood plants with swollen underground parts that act as reserve food stores.

Planting Plant your trees and shrubs singly and your herbaceous plants in groups of three or more. If you have any rose beds, plant a variety of rose to each bed – you will find that drifts of one colour are always more effective than dotting the colours here and there. Remember that certain combinations of shrubs flowering at approximately the same time look attractive if planted together; one example is a combination of shrubs such as *Cornus mas* 'Elegantissima', a variegated-leaved form of the Cornelian cherry, with yellow and pink leaves; *Prunus cerasifera* 'Atropurpurea' ('Pissardii'), the purple-leaf plum, almond and forsythia; *Potentilla fruticosa* and *Spiraea × bumalda* 'Anthony Waterer'; lilac and laburnum.

Below: *An informal corner, in which plants are grouped irregularly. A climbing plant has been used to disguise an ugly fence.*

Bedding plants

Botanical name	Colour	Height cm (ft)	Planting Distance cm (in)	Remarks
Ageratum	Mauve, blue, White	25 (¾)	15 (6)	Edging and small beds.
Alternanthera	Coloured foliage	8 (¼)	10–15 (4–6)	Edging.
Alyssum (sweet)	White, pink, lilac	20–30 (⅔–1)	10–15 (4–6)	Edging.
Amaranthus	Purple, dark red	60 (2)	30 (12)	Dot plants.
Antirrhinum	Various	15–45 (½–1½)	15–30 (6–12)	Best when massed.
Aster (annual)	Various	15–45 (½–1½)	15–30 (6–12)	Good for cutting.
Begonia (fibrous)	Pink, red and white	30 (1)	25 (9)	Good for small beds.
Begonia (tuberous)	Various	25–30 (¾–1)	25 (9)	Shady beds.
Calceolaria (shrubby)	Yellow, bronze	30 (1)	25 (9)	Well-drained soil.
Celosia argentea Cristata (cockcomb)	Red and yellow	30 (1)	25 (9)	Rich soil.
C.a. Plumosa	Red and yellow	60 (2)	25 (9)	Rich soil.
Centaurea candidissima	Silver leaves	25 (¾)	25 (9)	Provides a good foil.
Dahlia (small and medium)	Various	30–120 (1–4)	30–90 (12–36)	Needs a rich soil.
Echeveria	Grey leaved, succulent, sometimes edged bronze or red	30 (1)	15 (6)	Sunny dry soil.
Fuchsia	Pink, red or purple, white	30–120 (1–4)	45–90 (18–36)	Standard dot plants.
Gazania	Yellow, orange, purple-brown, often zoned	25–30 (¾–1)	25–30 (9–12)	Good for edging.
Godetia	Pink, white and crimson	15–60 (½–2)	25–30 (9–12)	Sunny position.
Heliotropium × hybridum	Purple, lilac, white	25–90 (¾–3)	25–120 (9–48)	Grows as a standard.
Iresine	Red or variegated leaves	30 (1)	25 (9)	Good foil plants.
Kochia	Green foliage, later red	60 (2)	45 (18)	Used as dot plants.
Lobelia	Blue, carmine, white	10 (⅓)	15 (6)	Edging.
Marguerite	White, yellow	45–60 (1½–2)	30–45 (12–18)	Sunny position.
Marigold (African and French)	Yellow, orange, crimson	15–60 (½–2)	15–30 (6–12)	Hot, dry soil.
Mesembryanthemum criniflorum	Various	tr	25 (9)	Full sun.
Nemesia	Various	25–30 (¾–1)	15 (6)	Best when massed.
Nicotiana	White, crimson, yellow	45–90 (1½–3)	30 (12)	Will grow in shade. Blooms open at night with heavy fragrance.
Pansies	Various	15 (½)	25 (9)	Edging or small beds.
Pelargonium (geranium)	Pink, red and white	45 (1½)	3 (12)	Sun or shade.
Pelargonium (ivy-leaved)	Pink, red and white	tr	45 (18)	Standards or dot plants.
Penstemon	Various	45 (1½)	30 (12)	Sun or shade.
Petunias	Various	10–30 (⅓–1)	30 (12)	Useful for shade.
Phlox drummondii	Various	25 (¾)	20–30 (8–12)	Best pegged down.
Salvia	Blue	45–60 (1½–2)	30 (12)	Sunny position.
Salvia	Scarlet	30–60 (1–2)	30 (12)	Sunny position.
Seneco maritima	Silver leaves	15–25 (½–¾)	15–25 (6–9)	Good foliage plant.
Stocks (10 week)	Various	30–60 (1–2)	30 (12)	Good rich soil.
Venidium	Various	60 (2)	45 (18)	Full sun.
Verbena	Various	tr	25–30 (9–12)	Edging.
Viola (pansy)	Various	15 (½)	25 (9)	Edging or small beds.
Zinnia	Various	25–60 (¾–2)	25–30 (9–12)	Full sun.

Key: tr = trailing

Rock gardens

Siting Most gardens should have a suitable situation for a rock garden as there are few hard and fast rules about siting. Ideally you should choose a gentle slope falling to the south or southwest, or as near as possible. Avoid a northeast aspect, as freezing winds can come from this quarter and harm many plants. If, however, these are unavoidable, some shelter can be afforded by planting shrubs and small trees on their windward side, but do not allow them to overhang the rock garden.

The site, however, must be well-drained. If it is likely to be waterlogged, drainage must be installed. As a rock garden is a decorative feature you might like it sited near the house or at least visible from it. Your choice of plants will also have an important bearing on its siting. Plants which enjoy a cool situation will obviously not live happily in the same conditions as those which thrive under a Mediterranean sun, so try to find a site which offers a wide variety of aspects, or you will find that you are limited in your choice of plants.

A steep bank or grassy slope, although difficult to mow, is a popular choice. Such a situation is ideal, because it can lend itself to the introduction of water, e.g. a waterfall and pool arrangement, which might enhance your rock garden's beauty.

Whenever possible use local stone for a rock garden, because it is more in keeping with the environment, particularly if your house, or garden wall, is built in the same kind of stone.

Limestone should be avoided near large towns, because polluted air produces hard, marble-like whiteness, which stands out harshly. If there is no local stone available to you and you have to buy one that is imported, choose natural stone. Avoid buying cheaper substitutes such as broken concrete, smashed masonry or bricks, as they will probably weather and have to be replaced. Another alternative would be to buy natural-looking, lightweight, man-made rocks which are available nowadays.

Soil If a rock garden is built on a flat site, considerably more soil will be needed than when it is on a slope. If no soil is readily obtainable, or the existing soil is poor, then you will have to buy it. A sunken, or partially sunken rock garden can be created by digging out one or more valley-shaped trenches, and piling the soil on either side to

Below left: *The beautiful blue Gentiana sino-ornata which looks best planted in a bright sunny position in the rock garden.*

Below right: *There are a great many cushion-forming plants in the rock garden. This is Saxifraga x jenkinsae, which is one of the earliest to flower.*

Bottom left: *Even the smallest rock garden can accommodate little conifers. Care should be taken to ensure that they are properly sited.*

Bottom right: *Dianthus 'Charles Musgrave', a rock garden plant, is representative of the old-fashioned pinks, which have adorned gardens for many years.*

Above left: *Lithospermum oleifolium is an attractive rock garden plant with deep blue flowers.*

Above right: *The alpine phlox adsurgens which thrives best in rich soil and on a sunny ledge in a rock garden.*

Top left: *Dianthus alpinus is a mat-forming plant which will tolerate a slightly acid soil.*

Top right: *'Riverslea' is a late-flowering aubrietia.*

create height. The site, of course, must be well drained.

For each tonne (ton) of stone you will need ¾ cubic metre (1 cubic yard) of compost. A suitable compost for most alpines consists of 4 parts, by bulk, good loam (top soil) preferably fibrous, to 2 parts peat or leaf mould and 1½ parts grit, which assists drainage. In places where you desire more choice plants the latter can be increased to 2 or 2½ parts. Before mixing, the compost ingredients should be dusted with 3.5 kilos (7lb) of bonemeal to ¾ cubic metre (1 cubic yard). The grit you use can be washed sharp sand but should not be builders' yellow sand.

These ingredients should be mixed thoroughly by turning them over a number of times. Then cover, to prevent the compost becoming wet or drying out, until it is needed. The formula can be varied to meet the needs of the plants you wish to grow. You can make your soil acid or alkaline by the addition of peat or lime respectively, so that it can be used in separate pockets made in the rockery, for the benefit of individual plants. Ready-made special purpose soil mixtures are available, but they are expensive.

Preparing the site Correct preparation of the site for a rockery is vital. To remedy mistakes later might mean major reconstruction work. The site must be drained if it is liable to become waterlogged, particularly when the soil is very heavy. Alpine plants do not like their roots to be in water. If the soil is good, you need only dig it over thoroughly, removing all weeds and their roots.

If you are intending to include a water feature, all pipe work, concrete channels and pools should be completed before building the rockery. Glass-fibre pools and plastic sheeting, however, can be incorporated during construction.

Designing the layout Before starting construction, draw a rough plan of your proposed rock garden, marking the positions of the principal features and paths, etc. Mark these out on the site with stakes. You cannot plan exactly where each stone goes, but it is important to arrange them in a natural manner so that the rockery blends in well with its surroundings. Study a few well-made rockeries to see how the rocks can be arranged.

The first rock or 'keystone' is always the most difficult to place. It is usually put at a bulge in the periphery with its front face slightly sloping backwards, and its strata running more or less horizontally. Every other rock is put down with the same backward slope, in close association with its neighbour.

It is easier to build a rock garden on a slope, as a flat site must first have the soil heaped up upon it and you have to use your imagination to create an illusion of peaks and valleys.

During construction it is important to remember that many alpines thrive best in narrow crevices between rocks.

As you will find it difficult to insert them after the work is finished, plant them during building. The main planting should be done later, when the compost has had time to settle.

Suggested plants

With a few exceptions alpines are not difficult to grow if they are given the right conditions. They are mostly tolerant of varying conditions, but might easily die if they are planted in sour and badly-drained soil, exposed to drips from overhanging trees, or exposed to cold draughts or winds. Avoid the temptation to include quick spreading plants (gross-growers) in your rockery, because they smother the slower-growing plants and become so strongly rooted that the rockery then has to be dismantled to dislodge them.

There are many attractive plants that are not strictly alpines that can be grown in a rock garden. Some *Acaena* species, for instance, are excellent for

Above: *Dianthus neglectus forms a dense mat and flowers in summer.*

Top: *A rock garden of warm sandstone. Early autumn is the best time to plan the display for the following season and to move plants from one place to another.*

Rock garden plants

Genus and Species or Cultivar	Colour	Description
Spring		
Alyssum ('Gold Dust')	Yellow	Grows to about 30cm (1 ft).
Arabis ('Rock Cress')	White, carmine red and pink	Grows best in a sunny place.
Aubrieta	Mauve, purple, red, rose-pink, violet	Hardy trailing evergreen perennials.
Gentiana acaulis (excisa)	Blue	Trumpet-like flowers.
Hypericum rhodopeum	Yellow, grey-green foliage	Gives a permanent effect.
Saxifraga 'Winston Churchill'	Pink	A 'mossy' saxifraga
Late spring		
Alpine Phlox	Blue, lavender-blue, magenta, pink, purple, red, rosy-red, salmon-pink, white	Grow well on ledges of rockeries.
Dianthus (Alpine Pinks)	Red, pink and white	Fragrant.
Dryas octopetala	White	Prostrate shrub: drapes its woody stems over the rocks.
Early summer		
Armeria maritima (Thrift) 'Vindictive' 'Bloodstone' 'Merlin'	Pink, red	Dwarf perennials.
Armeria maritima alba	White	Need a sunny position.
Helianthemum ('Sun roses')	Wide range of colours	Sub-shrubs. Enjoy a warm, dry situation.
Summer		
Achillea (Yarrow)	Yellow, white	Good carpeters.
Aethionema 'Warley Rose'	Rose	Dainty blue-green leaves.
Alyssum spinosum	White, pink	Spiny bushes.
Campanula species, hybrids and cultivars	Blue, violet, white	Some are fast-growing.
Gentiana septemfida	Bright blue	Hardy perennial.
Geranium cinereum	Red	Flowers in summer.
G. dalmaticum	Pink	Good ground cover.
G. renardii	White, delicately purple veined	Grey-green foliage.
G. subcaulescens	Cerise	Good ground cover.
Autumn		
Saxifraga fortunei	White	Handsome foliage.
Winter		
Saxifraga × jenkinsae	Pink	Cushion-forming plant.

Below: *Daboecia cantabrica, Irish or Connemara Heath, flowers during summer and autumn. Although it naturally lives in bog conditions it will grow quite well in a semi-shaded position and in light moist peaty soil.*

Bottom left: *Erica cinerea 'Coccinea', a cultivar (variety) of the Scotch or Bell Heather.*

Bottom right: *The common ling or heather, Calluna vulgaris. This evergreen bushy shrub blooms from summer to early autumn.*

carpeting, but are rampant growers and should not be planted close to small plants. They are also excellent for filling chinks in paved paths or as ground cover for bulbs in open areas.

Foliage plants are valuable in a rock garden and can be bought at garden centres. One is *Artemisia lanata (pedemonta)*, which has silver leaves and provides attractive ground cover.

Try to choose plants that give interest all the year around. One of the greatest faults of many rock gardens is that they look beautiful in spring but are dull for the rest of the year. The table on page 19 suggests some easy-to-grow rock garden plants that will jointly give colour from spring to late winter.

Heather gardens

There is a mistaken belief that all heaths and heathers are lime-haters. It is true that *Calluna vulgaris* and its cultivars and most of the ericas and daboecia must have a lime-free soil, but *Erica carnea, E. × darleyensis, E. erigena (E. mediterranea)* and *E. stricta* and their cultivars will thrive in soil containing some lime. Therefore, you can grow these delightful hardy shrubs in ordinary garden soil. It should be noted, however, that all heaths and heathers dislike a heavy clay soil.

The avoidance of rich soils too is important, as these shrubs become straggly and do not flower properly if given over-rich conditions. Peat is excellent for heathers and should be worked into the soil before planting is started. It may be used as a top dressing to help retain moisture which is so necessary for these plants. They also need sunny situations and flourish on exposed, high ground. Although heathers do best in a moist soil, a waterlogged site must be avoided at all costs.

One of the many virtues of these evergreen shrubs is that by careful selection it is possible to have variations in flower colour, ranging from white through pink and purple to deep mauve, throughout the year. Colour, too, is provided by the foliage in many shades of green, silvery and grey-green, copper and gold and, in addition, some kinds take on brightly coloured hues in the winter. The colours of dwarf conifers too will mix well with heaths.

Planting Heathers are extremely adaptable and have many uses. For the best effect plant three or more plants of each variety in a group. These patches of colour can be placed at the front of a shrub or mixed border, or act as ground cover among taller shrubs. The rock garden is an ideal place for heathers, or they can be grown in exposed positions in the garden where little else will battle against the cold winds. They make decorative low hedges and are excellent for covering unsightly banks, as the slope of a bank ensures good drainage. As ground cover plants for open positions the heaths and heathers are unsurpassable – they spread easily and smother any weeds. When used for this purpose they should be planted fairly closely together.

Planting can take place, if weather conditions are suitable, at any time from early autumn to spring. It is best to plant with a trowel and make sure that there are no long bare stems visible. The foliage should come right down to ground level. Heathers dislike hard, unyielding soil, so prepare the site well before beginning to plant and break down any hard lumps.

Heathers can easily be kept under control by simply clipping off all the old flowered spikes in early spring. This treatment is all that is necessary, unless they have been neglected, in which case the long, straggly stems will need shortening back.

Conifers

If you wish to grow conifers in your garden, you must be sure that you choose ones that are slow-growing. With the increasing popularity of the rock garden during the present century, it has been realized that dwarf conifers, with their great variety in form, colour and texture, not only provide a suitable background for small alpine plants but also furnish and carpet the bare rock work throughout the long season when there is little in flower. As features in a small garden conifers are both attractive and labour saving. They should not, however, be used to excess.

The following list gives a selection. When they grow to more than 30–60cm (1–2ft) in height, their ultimate dimensions are given. Some will have to be obtained from nurseries that specialize in rock garden and alpine plants.

Conical and pyramidal: *Cedrus libani* 'Nana'; *Chamaecyparis obtusa* 'Nana Pyramidalis'; *Juniperus communis* 'Compressa'; *Picea glauca albertiana* 'Conica'; *Thuja plicata* 'Rogersii'.

Spreading and flat-topped: *Cedrus libani* 'Sargent'; *Chamaecyparis lawsoniana* 'Lycopodioides'; *C. obtusa* 'Lycopodioides', to 3m (9ft); *C. o.* 'Nana'; *C. o.* 'Pygmaea'; *C. pisifera* 'Squarrosa Intermedia'; *Cryptomeria japonica* 'Pygmaea'; *Juniperus communis nana; J. horizontalis*, prostrate dwarf, wide spreading; *J. x media* 'Pfitzeriana'; *J. sabina tamariscifolia*, grows in layers, spreads vigorously; *J. squamata* 'Meyeri'; *Picea abies* 'Gregoryana'; *P. a.* 'Nidiformis'; *P. a.* 'Repens' wide spreading; *Podocarpus alpinus*, *P. nivalis*.

Erect: *Chamaecyparis lawsoniana* 'Ellwoodii', to 3m (9ft); *C. l.* 'Gimbornii'; *C. l.* 'Mimima'. *Pinus sylvestris* 'Beuvronensis', miniature Scots pine of open, erect growth.

Globular: *Chamaecyparis lawsoniana* 'Forsteckensis'. *Cryptomeria japonica* 'Globosa Nana'; *C. j.* 'Vilmoriniana'; *Juniperus chinensis* 'Blaauw's Variety'; *Picea mariana* 'Nana'.

Coloured foliage: *Chamaecyparis lawsoniana* 'Lutea Nana', erect, golden; *C. l.* 'Minima Aurea', pyramidal, golden; *C. l.* 'Pygmaea Argentea', globose, shoots tipped silver; *Chamaecyparis obtusa* 'Lycopodioides Aurea', lax, to 2.5m (8ft). *Chamaecyparis pisifera* 'Filifera Aurea', low bush, bright yellow; *C. p.* 'Plumosa Compressa', flat-topped, golden. *Juniperus x media* 'Pfitzerana Aurea' spreading, golden.

Trellis-work and pergolas

Trellis-work, besides being an interesting feature in a small garden, enables you to secure privacy and shelter. It can be obtained either in a horizontal or

Above: *Chamaecyparis lawsoniana 'Stewartii' is a beautiful, golden-coloured conifer which can make an attractive feature if you have room for it.*

Top: *There are a variety of different shapes and sizes of conifers. If you wish to include these features in your garden take care not to use them to excess, so that each one can be appreciated.*

21

diagonal pattern. As a decorative support for climbers it can provide shelter from the wind, or afford some shade if the sun is strong. The beauty of it is that it gives a feeling of space beyond it. It can be fixed to the top of a wall or fence, or to the surface of a plain brick wall or can be made to stand alone.

Making trellis fencing You can make your own trellis, if you are good at woodwork. Obtain laths measuring from 2.5cm x 6mm (1in x ¼in) to 5.0cm x 2.5cm (2in x 1in) thick, depending on the weight required. The timber should be treated with preservative.

The laths should be fastened together vertically and horizontally to form a mesh of 15cm x 20cm (6in x 8in) squares. They should be fixed together with 20mm or 25mm (¾in or 1in) long galvanized nails, driven through the wood against a clout plate. The trellis

Right: *Trellis-work of wood or plastic is invaluable for screening purposes, but should be firmly fixed, otherwise it may get blown over in strong winds. The trellis here is covered in ivy and would effectively screen an unsightly view.*

Below left: *Climbing roses are especially suitable for pergolas. 'Chaplin's Pink Companion', which blooms over a fairly long period, has silvery-pink flowers.*

Below centre: *A firm support for a climbing plant can be provided by a stout trellis attached to a wall. As the base of a wall is dry, plants should be planted about 38cm (15in) in front of it and supported by a cane sloping towards it, until the growth is tall enough to be tied to the trellis.*

Below right: *When a trellis has to support growth of heavy weight, for instance, roses, it is wise to erect its uprights in a base of concrete.*

is best constructed in manageable panels and fixed directly to supports already driven into the ground or, for heavy duty, fixed to a framework of 2.5cm or 4cm (1in or 1½in) square. Long lengths of trellis should be supported on 5cm (2in) square or 5cm x 8cm (2in x 3in) timber uprights placed at intervals of 1m (3ft) to 2m (6ft), according to the exposure to wind. Trellis-work fitted to walls should be attached to small wooden blocks fixed to the wall, to allow air circulation and the plants to clamber in and out.

It is possible to buy ready-made panels of varying sizes or 'ready to assemble' kits.

Pergolas
Pergolas usually take the form of either a series of arches, which, when erected over a pathway provide an attractive covered walk, or a single row of uprights, cross-pieces and 'fill in' pieces which make an attractive pattern.

Various materials can be used in their construction. Larch or pine are very popular timbers, as oak or cedarwood can be very expensive. Remember to treat the timbers with preservative before construction. It is possible to purchase 'do-it-yourself' pergola kits, which are comprised of accurately machined and cut components that fit easily together. You can construct an elegant pergola with brick or stone uprights and sawn cross-members, or a rustic one which will be less sophisticated. Choose a style to suit your garden. A pergola can form an attractive feature in the middle of the lawn, act as a divider between, say, a flower and vegetable garden, form a covered walk, or hide an unsightly view.

Suggested plants
Pergolas and trellis-work are both suitable structures for climbing and trailing plants, the main drawback being that in these cases the plants need more pruning than when grown elsewhere.

If you want your trellis to form a screen, clothe it with densely foliaged plants. Here are a few suggestions.
Clematis montana. A quick and very hardy climber with pink or white flowers.
Cobaea scandens (Cup and saucer plant). An invaluable annual climber that will grow to a considerable height in one season, with either deep blue or green flowers. It can be grown in shady places.
Ipomoea tricolor (Morning Glory). A

pretty annual climber with bright blue flowers which must have sun.
Lonicera japonica (Japanese Honeysuckle). A totally or semi-evergreen fast-growing climber with white and yellow sweet-smelling flowers. *L. j.* 'Aureoreticulata' has leaves with a pattern of golden veins.
Polygonum baldschuanicum (Russian vine). A particularly fast-growing climber which should only be grown if you have a vast area to cover.
Rosa (Rose). There are many different sorts of climbing rose, so choose one that suits the aspect.
Parthenocissus (quinquefolia) (Virginia creeper). This is one of the best-known species which has beautifully coloured red autumnal leaves.

Supports for climbers
Some climbers are self-clinging, whilst others need some support (see page 36). This can be in the form of occasional ties or wire netting, which should be wound loosely around the uprights of the trellis or pergola to provide something to which the plants can cling. The ties or wire netting will quickly be hidden by the growths of the more vigorous climbers, e.g. akebias, ampelopsis, *Aristolochia macrophylla,* clematis, eccremocarpus, jasminum, lathyrus, lonicera, parthenocissus, periploca, passiflora, roses, vitis or wisteria.

When training plants against trellis-work and pergolas, you should use soft materials, such as raffia, string or plastic-coated wire (depending on the weight of the plant) to tie them in place.

If you are fixing your trellis to a wall, remember that twining or clinging plants are easier to manage than those with branches that need continual support. If, however, you choose the former type of plant it is better not to paint the trellis, because it is impossible to extricate the plant when repainting becomes necessary.

Insulated wire or plastic clothes lines, fixed by vine eyes about 5cm (2in) from the wall, provide a good alternative to a trellis for supporting climbers.

Above: *Morning Glory, the common name of Ipomoea tricolor, is a half-hardy annual climber. It is excellent as a temporary covering for a wall while the more permanent plants are growing.*

Top left: *The initial tying of a plant to a trellis is made mid-way along the plant growth, not at the tip. For this purpose raffia string or plastic-coated wire should be used.*

Top right: *Fix trellis-work to the wall with Rawlplugs, using old cotton reels as distance pieces.*

Herbs and herb gardens

Herbs can be grown in small gardens in the crevices in paving, in ornamental beds or in a segregated herb garden. Some of the thymes suitable for planting in paving are the prostrate forms of *Thymus drucei (serpyllum)*. *T. d. lanugingosus* is one which quickly forms a dense carpet of grey woolly foliage.

Herbs can be successfully planted amongst flowers in your garden, and some are particularly attractive or sweet-smelling. *Artemisia abrotanum*, known variously as lad's love, southernwood and old man, is a herb whose aromatic foliage has always been enjoyed by country folk and if you have an old house you may find it growing in strategic positions, at the junction of paths or by the kitchen door. *Lavandula spica*, the old English lavender, is a popular choice because of its fragrance.

Thymes are obtainable in great variety – the soft lavender flowers of the lemon thyme, *Thymus × citriodorus* 'Silver Queen', make an attractive contrast to its silver-variegated foliage.

Herb gardens

If you decide to have a herb garden it need not be large, but should be enclosed or in a sheltered position with the plants spaced out. On hot days you will find that the aromatic scent of the herbs drifts through the whole garden.

Any herb garden, whether it is a simple border or a complicated knot garden, needs careful thought. You must know about the heights and growing habits of the plants, otherwise your tall subjects may be planted in the front of the bed or next to, and smothering, the short or creeping herbs. Beware planting *Artemisia dracunculus* (tarragon) and *Mentha* (mint) in a mixed herb bed, as they tend to take over, strangling everything else. Try to keep them separate, or put slates down into the soil to stop their roots from creeping over into the rest of the bed.

When planning a garden think too about which herbs like sun and which are happier in dappled shade. Generally speaking *Origanum* (marjoram), *Rosmarinus officinalis* (rosemary), *Salvia officinalis* (sage) and *Thymus* (thyme), need a lot of sun and can stand dryness, while the juicier green herbs such as *Allium schoenoeprasum* (chives), *Anthriscus cerefolium* (chervil), and *Mentha* (mint) prefer a moist spot and some shade. Herb gardens must look neat and be accessible, so if the garden is big enough they are best arranged in plots divided by paths of stone, brick, gravel or creeping thyme, or *Mentha pulegium*. Individual herbs may be separated similarly. Hedges of lavender can also act as dividers, but will need regular clipping.

Sowing Herbs need a sheltered south-facing plot, where the soil is well-drained, but providing it is not too heavy, they will grow in almost any soil.

The soil should be well dug and limed in autumn, dug again in spring and raked to make a seed bed. Some herbs are sown from seed, either in their permanent growing quarters, where they are ultimately thinned out, or in boxes to be transplanted when large enough. If you have a greenhouse or frame you can sow many annuals earlier and have them ready to put out when the danger of frost has passed. During dry periods seedlings should be well-watered. Keeping your herb garden free of weeds is also important.

Many herbs, both annuals and perennials, can be bought as plants, but remember to label perennial herbs so that they can be found again after they have died down in winter.

Herbs

Common and botanical name	Approx. ultimate height cm (in)	Remarks
Sun-loving		
Balm, Lemon (P) *(Melissa officinalis)*	60–90 (24–36)	Easy to grow.
Basil, Sweet (A) *(Ocimum basilicum)*	60–90 (24–36)	Sweetly aromatic leaves.
Borage (R) *(Borago officinalis)*	45–60 (18–24)	Has a cucumber-like fragrance and lovely blue flowers. Easy to grow.
Garlic (P) *(Allium Sativum)*	30-60 (12–24)	Attractive in a flower border.
Hyssop (SS) *(Hyssopus officinalis)*	60–120 (24–48)	Quite hardy and is perennial. Leaves have a bitter minty flavour.
Marjoram, Sweet (SS) *(Origanum majorana)*	60 (24)	Grown as an annual. Needs protection from frost in cold districts.
Marjoram, Pot (P) *(Origanum onites)*	30 (12) 60 (24) in flower	Aromatic foliage. Needs winter-covering against frost in cold areas.
Rosemary (S) *(Rosmarinus officinalis)*	90–150 (36–60)	Prefers chalky soil. R. officinalis 'Prostata' is a smaller variety, reaching 15–20 cm (6–8 in).
Rue (S) *(Ruta graveolens 'Jackman's Blue')*	60–90 (24–36)	Most attractive border plant with its aromatic, blue-green leaves. Grows well in chalky soil.
Sage (SS) *(Salvia officinalis 'Aureo-variegata')*	60 (24)	Grows best in light, chalky soil. An attractive plant, needing little attention.
Salad Burnet (P) *(Sanguisorba minor)*	40 (15)	Easy to grow. Prefers chalky soil.
Savory, Summer (A) *(Satureja hortensis)*	30 (12)	Strongly aromatic leaves. Excellent in rockeries or borders.
Savory, Winter (P) *(Satureja montana)*	30 (12)	Although perennial, develops a woody base and is better replaced every two or three years.
Southernwood (S) *(Artemisia abrotanum)*	60–120 (24–48)	Attractive shrub for a border, with greyish, divided, aromatic leaves.
Thyme (P) *(Thymus drucei)*	8 (3)	Grows in chalky soil.
Thyme, Lemon (P) *(Thymus x citrio dorus)*	10–15 (4–6)	Lemon-scented. Grows in chalky soil.
Sun- or partial shade-loving		
Bergamot (P) *(Monarda didyma)*	60–90 (24–36)	Requires moist soil. Attracts bees and butterflies.
Chives (P) *(Allium schoenoprasum)*	15–25 (6–10)	Will grow in chalky soil full of humus. Easy to grow. Attractive pale purple flowers.
Costmary (P) *(Chrysanthemum balsamita)*	90 (36)	Aromatic when bruised.
Parsley (B) *(Petroselinum crispum)*	30–60 (12–24)	Good edging to borders. Protected with cloches gives winter supplies.
Sun- or shade-loving		
Sorrel, French (P) *(Rumex scutatus)*	30–45 (12–18)	Easy to grow.
Sweet Cicely (P) *(Myrrhus odorata)*	60–90 (24–36)	Remarkable for its sweet and highly aromatic foliage.
Shade-loving		
Mint (P) *(Mentha spicata)*	60 (24)	Easy to grow. Apple Mint (M. rotundifolia) and Eau de Cologne Mint (A variety of M. citrata) are other alternatives.

Key:
A: Annual, B: Biennial, P: Perennial,
S: Shrub, SS: Sub-shrub.

Below: *Parsley, Petroselinum crispum, is a decorative biennial. The seeds take from six to eight weeks to germinate and the plant prefers partial shade and needs to be well-watered in hot weather.*

Bottom: *The colourful flowers of chives (Allium shoenoprasum), which are pale mauve to purple or pink, make it an attractive plant to grow in a herb garden.*

Above left: *Plum 'Czar', an old favourite cultivar (variety), should be pruned to an upward growing bud.*

Above right: *A well-laid out vegetable garden which has been fully-developed to give the fullest supply of produce from a small plot.*

Right: *The Globe Artichoke is a vegetable growing in popularity, as it can be grown decoratively in the rear of a mixed border.*

Kitchen gardens

Due to the high cost of vegetables and fruit today, many people are starting to grow their own. Starting a kitchen garden in a small area is not impossible but it does need careful planning.

If you are very short of space you may be consoled in the thought that you can still grow vegetables and fruit, without digging up your lawn, because quite a number of fairly common vegetables are ornamental and look very attractive growing among flowers.

Produce among flowers

Runner beans have pretty scarlet flowers and can look gay in a border, climbing a wigwam of bamboo canes. Patrons of Chinese restaurants may be surprised to know that their favourite chop suey green is none other than the annual chrysanthemum, with its bright daisy-like flowers, masquerading under another name.

Some of the more common vegetables, such as carrots and beetroot, have foliage pretty enough to compete with any ornamental plants, and a lush ring of lettuce looks attractive in the front of an herbaceous border. Other suitable ornamental vegetables are the tall-growing, majestic globe artichokes with their grey leaves and thistle-like edible heads. Trailing marrows, such as 'Long White', can be made to climb a fence, but you must support the weight of the marrows in net bags.

The outdoor climber 'Kyoto' is a cultivar (variety) of cucumber particularly suitable for this type of garden, as is the increasingly popular vegetable, salsify, which was formerly grown in gardens solely for the impressive appearance of its foliage.

Moreover, this style of growing food is not confined to vegetables. Apple and pear blossom are very decorative, but if you choose to grow them make sure that your garden centre supplies you with bushes grafted on to dwarf stock. Dwarf apricots too can be obtained, reaching a height of only 60–90cm (2–3ft). A 1.5m (5ft) hedge can be grown within 12 months from raspberry canes, which will give you 10kgs (20lbs) of delicious raspberries. Blackberries are a very effective screen for an ugly shed, and so are loganberries.

Kitchen gardens

If you have a larger-sized 'small garden' you may feel that, rather than jumbling vegetables and flowers together, you would prefer to have a separate vegetable and fruit garden. Decide on its size and site first – how much space you can spare and whether you want it to be easily accessible from the house or out of sight from your windows. Trellis-work will provide effective screening for this purpose.

Intensive cultivation If you have very little room to spare you will need to get the highest possible yield from your ground. This means you must practise intensive cultivation. Prepare the soil in the area well, maintain high fertility and keep weeds down, because otherwise the latter will absorb the food and water intended for the crops.

When you know how much space you can devote to a kitchen garden you should dig the soil deeply – up to 30cm (12in) on a fine autumn day, or later if it is more convenient and there is no frost. Add well-made compost, peat or well-rotted farmyard or stable manure. Unless the soil is limy or chalky, dress the surface with a small handful of lime per 930 sq cm (1 sq ft) in the first year. Repeat every third year at half this rate.

Just before you plant out in spring distribute general fertilizer at the rate recommended by the maker. Do not forget to keep the ground well-watered all the time.

Vegetables

Another decision you will need to make before preparing a site for a kitchen garden, is the kind and quantity of vegetables you wish to grow, as this will have direct bearing on the amount of space you need. You might decide to rule out potatoes as they are relatively cheap today. On the other hand, you may choose to grow a row of new potatoes, or salad or continental sorts.

Having considered your family's preferences, you must work out, for each vegetable, how many meals you wish to cater for and for how long. If you have a deep-freeze then you must also consider its storage space.

Having drawn up a schedule of your requirements, it is possible to work out approximately the minimum amount of space you will need in your garden for vegetables, taking into account successional sowings. If you look at books on vegetable growing or seedsmen's catalogues, they usually include suggestions regarding spacing. For example, one supplier recommends ultimately thinning out parsnips so that the rows are 38cm (15in) apart and the plants are 21cm (8in) apart. This means that four parsnips are planted in every 930 sq cm (1 sq ft). Similarly it is recommended that lettuces should be ultimately thinned out to 30cm (12in) apart, in rows that are also 30cm (12in) apart – so two lettuces will require an area of 930 sq cm (1 sq ft).

By equating these calculations with your total requirements for the period you will be able to decide the total area that you will need to devote to vegetables. You should also allow 30cm (1ft) all round the total area to lessen the risk of any plants spreading themselves over the adjoining lawn or paths. A booklet has been published by a leading horticultural chemical manufacturer which will help you make these calculations.

Fruit

There are two main types of fruit – top fruit, e.g. apples, pears, plums – and soft fruit, e.g. gooseberries, currants, raspberries and the climbers, blackberries, loganberries and hybrids.

If you wish to include top fruit in your garden, you will be able to grow apples, pears and plums, provided that they are cultivars (varieties) grafted on dwarf rootstocks (unfortunately there is no such rootstock for cherries), but they need to have other cultivars close by to pollinate them. This might make further demands on your limited space. This problem, in the case of apples, has been overcome, to some extent, by the introduction of the family apple tree, which makes it possible to graft, for instance, two dessert and one cooking cultivar on to a common rootstock to save space. The same applies to pears.

The most popular way of growing apples, pears and plums in a small garden is as cordons, fan-trained or espalier trees which, besides being

Above: *Apricots can be grown on a sunny wall where the radiated heat from the bricks provides extra warmth, protecting the blossom and encouraging ripening.*

Top: *A triple cordon apple grown against a wall to utilize a small space. Equally it could be trained against a trellis to make a division. Plums and pears can also be grown in the same way.*

Above: *If your house is set high above the road a rockery makes an original front garden. Shallow rocks have been used here for informal steps, which have become overgrown with fast-spreading rock plants.*

Top: *A front garden with flower beds lining the drive, which have been planted with allyssum, lobelia, candytuft, dwarf nasturtiums and French marigolds.*

productive, also make useful screening fences. In a similar way, soft fruit, such as gooseberries and red and white currants, need not be grown as bushes, which are space consuming, because all three can be obtained as cordons. The gooseberry 'Whinham's Industry' can be bought as a standard. Blackberries, loganberries and outdoor grapes can be grown on trellis-work to form screens.

Front gardens

Many front gardens today are laid out on traditional lines – a small lawn surrounded by a flower border and rose trees, with perhaps a centre bed. Your main aim, when planning your front garden, should be to make the greatest use of space without creating a boring layout. There are a number of ways to make it more interesting, however small or awkwardly shaped.

Paths and paving

Often the path to the front door is made of concrete which has become cracked, detracting from the beauty of the garden. In this case you could lay a crazy paving path, banked on either side with York sandstone, planting rock plants in the crevices.

One way of improving the appearance of a front garden is to position the front gate so that it is not directly opposite the front door and lay a curving path. If a straight path is essential, you might consider turning your front garden into a formal rose garden, because it is seldom possible to find space for such a charming feature elsewhere on a small plot. On the other hand, if the front garden slopes down or up steeply to the road, you could terrace it instead.

If you have little time or inclination for gardening you might consider paving the front garden with a natural stone like York, or even concrete paving slabs. Care should be taken in using coloured slabs, which are also available, because they can look garish. It might be better to choose grey slabs with perhaps an inset of colour. Plants in containers and hanging baskets around the door will also help to brighten a paved front garden.

Plants, rockeries and pools

In a very small front garden you should use vertical structures such as trellis-work, garden walls, house walls, fences and screens as supports for climbing plants and as focal points. See page 36 for information on climbing plants.

When designing your small front garden you could consider filling it with plants. Aim at having a lot of colourful flowers at eye level, or just below. Window boxes at first floor level can also be very effective. If you concentrate purely on flower beds at ground level you will emphasize the restricted space and make the garden look tiny.

Small rockeries can look very attractive in a front garden with a lawn. They will also act as outcrops from a flat paved garden and give a feeling of restfulness. See page 17 for hints on construction and a list of suitable plants.

Pools, which can look beautiful in a back garden, are not usually a good idea in front gardens. The proximity of the street can make them liable to become receptacles for litter blowing about. They are also a great attraction to other people's children thus being dangerous as well as a nuisance.

Flower beds

If you wish to have flower beds in your front garden the same rules apply as for those in back gardens. If you decide to construct flower beds on different levels, you will need to remove the topsoil and lay a foundation of hardcore to form the shape of a miniature landscape. The topsoil must then be replaced. As there will be a greater surface to cover you will need to provide more topsoil – either bought or taken from your back garden. Some form of paving between the beds will be not only decorative but essential, as you should have a firm area to walk on when planting or weeding the beds. **Raised beds** could also be constructed in a front garden. Their retaining edges can be made of either wood or stone. Raised beds help to overcome the problem of excessive wetness of the ground during the winter months. For lime-hating plants a raised peat bed supported by peat walls is attractive in appearance and easy to plant. Where space permits and there is a natural slope, raised peat beds make a charming setting for many ericaceous plants, such as gaultherias, dwarf rhododendrons, and heathers, and also for hardy ferns, ramondas, trilliums, dwarf astilbes and many other delightful hardy plants. These types of bed are particularly suitable for invalid gardeners, who can cultivate them in a wheelchair, or for those who find stooping troublesome.

Above: *Raised beds can be constructed in a front garden, with their retaining edges made of either wood or stone.*

Above centre: *A lych-gate, forming an effective eye-catching feature, which could be framed by climbing roses to add bright colour to it.*

Above left: *A suitable path for a small front garden. In order to minimize the growth of weeds, the joints between the crazy stones should be cemented. Small pockets can be left to accommodate the types of rock plants that can be trodden on without being harmed.*

Left: *A part of a front garden, which has been designed so that pots filled with ivy, geraniums and climbing and bush roses frame the porch.*

The town garden

Below: *A walled garden brightened with fuchsias, busy-lizzie, begonias and geraniums.*

Below centre: *A paved town garden used entirely for sitting out.*

Far right, top: *Statues form the focal points in this rectangular town garden.*

Far right, centre: *Using a mirror can achieve a sense of length and spaciousness.*

Far right, bottom: *A sophisticated town garden.*

In towns the word 'garden' is often misleading. The American term 'yard' might be more descriptive. Many back gardens are square or rectangular patches, often no more than 4.5 m (15 ft) wide.

Some of the most beautiful gardens in Britain are the walled and paved gardens of Georgian and Victorian houses with their fine trees and specially selected flowers in their sheltered beds. Today many town gardens are quadrangles incorporated in new architect-designed housing complexes. Whether old or new, these mini-gardens have different problems and rewards from other types of small gardens.

Firstly, you must decide whether you prefer to pave your garden, either wholly or partly, or lay a lawn. For a garden smaller than say, 24 sq m (260 sq ft) paving is generally more suitable and less work to maintain than a lawn. In a tiny town garden, particularly when it has a lot of use, an area could be entirely devoted to a play space for children (perhaps including a sandpit) or to sitting out or sunbathing.

Paved town gardens

When choosing paving stones for your garden it is better to keep to neutral grey or natural coloured slabs, thus

letting the flowers and foliage of bedding perennials, planted in borders and geometrically-shaped beds, provide the brighter colour.

Paving materials The use of contrasting materials in a paved garden can be very attractive, for example a sunburst of brick around a tree, a heather-brown quarry-tiled patio area near the house, or an outline of old-fashioned cobble stones to the paving itself. You might find mellow old bricks from a house that is being demolished or converted, which will provide an attractive alternative to cement or concrete. To make the yard look more informal you can plant at random between the paving stones. Do not forget that good drainage must be ensured in a paved garden. You can do this by making a slight incline towards a central drain or a few joints filled with gravel.

Focal points

All tiny gardens need a good focal point, such as a tree, water, plants or statuary to remove the impression of standing in a small square box. A tree for this purpose should either be an evergreen or have a good shape, even when bare. A sundial, or birdbath, placed on the edge of a raised bed, are two other eye-catching features.

Statuary, which can mean anything from an exquisite small bronze to a stone urn, heightens interest in any garden, particularly as such objects are often seen at their best out-of-doors. A raised garden pool makes another attractive feature.

Many other smaller items enhance a small space, ranging from a sundial brought from an old house to a fibreglass replica of an eighteenth-century urn. A Mediterranean look may be introduced with coloured pieces of Italian glass or ceramics, for instance an alcove could be lined with blue glass mosaic tiles or a ledge covered with ceramic tiles.

Using mirrors to give length is another effective idea – try a tall one to reflect a narrow little cypress. A square one could be put behind an urn of trailing geraniums or behind a wide-spaced trellis supporting blue morning glories. Even groups of chimney-pots or variously-sized drainpipes, draped in ivy or geraniums, can make decorative and colourful features and focal points.

A dramatic effect from the interplay of light and shadow can be created by installing flood-lighting in a small garden. You could put a lamp beneath the house wall shining on the plants opposite, at ground level behind a statue to throw it and the surrounding shrubs into relief, or set in a flower bed to illuminate a special feature or a particularly choice flower.

Conifers and miniature trees

In small town gardens conifers and miniature trees in containers can look very attractive and provide an alternative to formal flower beds. One of the conifers suitable for small gardens is the low-growing, wide-spreading *Juniperus x media* 'Pfitzeriana', with its branches bearing grey-green foliage, thrusting out at an angle of 45 degrees. Its ultimate height and spread are 2m (6ft) and 4m (12ft). Another is the prostrate *J. x media* 'Kosteri' which has plumose, grey-green ascending branches. *J.* 'Grey Owl' is lighter and more feathery. Both of these are approximately 1m (3ft) tall and 3.5m (10ft) across.

Several forms of *J. communis* are even more restricted. *J. c.* 'Prostata' 'Hornibrookii' is wide-spreading with green and silver foliage. It is good ground cover and takes the shape of the objects it engulfs. Low-growing *J. c.* 'Repanda' has branches packed with deep green needles that spread all round.

Others that make excellent ground cover are *J. horizontalis* 'Bar Harbor', the bright green carpeter, *J. procumbens* 'Nana' and *J. sabina tamariscifolia* with its grey feathery foliage which turns green on maturity.

The elegant and small-growing Japanese maples, *Acer palmatum* 'Dissectum Atropurpureum' and *A. p.* 'D. Palmatifidum' with their finely cut foliage contrast well with the darker coloured conifers. They are somewhat gnarled like bonsai. They thrive in partial shade. The dwarf rhododendrons, 'Bluebird', 'Blue Tit', 'Carmen' and 'Elizabeth', will flourish in acid soil, and are as colourful as their taller counterparts.

Bonsai

Bonsai, a Japanese word meaning 'trees growing in shallow containers', is the art of growing miniature trees. Bonsai are kept small by pruning and by being kept in a small container which restricts their root growth. Those grown over 60cm (2ft) are usually left outdoors, and so are suitable for town gardens, back yards or patios.

In general the best choice for bonsai are the slow-growing or small trees with small leaves or needles, small flowers and small fruit. Blooms, however, are never dwarfed and can look incongruous on a miniature tree if they are proportionately large. Evergreens are very popular and vary little from season to season.

Many trees which are not usually regarded as bonsai, can be successfully grown in miniature form. Before you

attempt to do this, determine the habits and soil preferences of the tree you choose, because you will improve your chances of success if you provide the right growing conditions.

Among excellent hardy subjects for bonsai treatment are the maples, *Acer palmatum* and *A. pseudoplatanus* (sycamore), both with attractive deciduous leaves; the cornelian cherry (*Cornus mas*) which is a deciduous tree, with clusters of yellow flowers in early spring, followed by red fruit; and the crab apple (*Malus*) which has either red or white blooms in early summer and colourful fruit in autumn.

Suitable evergreens are some of the cotoneasters, with their small leaves and berries; the juniper (*Juniper communis*) which has very small leaves; *Pyracantha coccinea* (firethorn), which has small leaves, white flowers and red berries and pine (*Pinus*), the most popular of bonsai and also the Japanese symbol of life.

Other trees that can be successfully grown as bonsai are:—

Evergreen: the false cypress (*Chamaecyparis*); the common spruce (*Picea abies*) and yew (*Taxus*).
Deciduous: Silver birch (*Betula*), beech (*Fagus*); boxthorn (*Lycium*); *Prunus* (Japanese cherry); apricot (*Prunus mume*); almond (*P. dulcis*); oak (*Quercus*); weeping willow (*Salix babylonica*); the mulberry (*Morus alba* and *nigra*) and lime (*Tilia x europaea*).

There are two ways of obtaining bonsai – either buying or growing them yourself. They are either sold growing

in a container or 'root-wrapped' in winter. This means they are sold with their root-ball protectively wrapped, and you can plant them in containers of your choice. Growing your own bonsai from seed, seedling or cutting is much cheaper, but will take far longer. Oak, beech, willow, sycamore and conifers are easily grown if they have sufficient warmth, moisture and air.

Fruit and vegetables

The rules for growing fruit and vegetables in a town garden are much the same as those outlined on page 26. However, if you pave the whole of your garden you will need to find other means of growing your own produce.

Summer fruiting or perpetual strawberries can be grown by cutting 5cm (2in) diameter holes in an old barrel, filling it with soil, and planting strawberry plants through the holes. To meet this intensive cultivation, the soil should be moisture-retaining and

Opposite page, top: *Drainage holes must be cut in the base of a strawberry barrel.*

Opposite page, bottom: *A bonsai, Juniperus chinensis.*

Above left: *Tomatoes and other vegetables can be grown in containers.*

Above right: *Fan-trained fig trees should be planted in a 62cm (2ft) deep and 95cm (3ft) wide hole and lined with brick or concrete blocks.*

Top left: *This paved town garden relies on foliage for colour.*

Top right: *Rhododendrons here are flowering in both tubs and beds made in the informal crazy paving.*

Below: *Tagetes patula 'Dainty Marietta' is a sparkling annual which flowers during the summer. It thrives as well in a container as in flower beds.*

Bottom: *A tranquil garden in the heart of a town with a grass walk between the flower beds, which have been filled with herbaceous and annual plants.*

rich. A good mixture is 7 parts, by volume, loam, 3 parts peat and 2 parts sand. To every 41kg (1 bushel) of the mixture 225 grams (9oz) of good general fertilizer should be added.

To grow strawberries in this way you will need to acquire either a barrel, which can be bought already cut, or an earthenware jar with holes. Mount barrels on casters as this allows them to be moved so that the fruit is evenly exposed to sun. Good cultivars of strawberries for barrels are 'Royal Sovereign' and 'Cambridge Vigour'.

Remember that strawberries need copious watering, especially after planting, and that water tends to escape through the uppermost holes. Good drainage is essential. After the first year feed them with a low-nitrogen/high-potash liquid manure. No training is necessary and the fruit can be protected against birds by a cage.

Other fruits, such as apples, pears, gooseberries and redcurrants can be grown in town gardens as cordons or espaliers against a wall. Gooseberries and redcurrants are also available as standards. Dwarf apricots grow well in tubs. A fig tree is an excellent choice because it needs to have its roots restricted to fruit well and thrives well in soil in a hole broken in the hardcore, providing the drainage is good.

Some smaller vegetables, such as carrots, lettuce, beetroot and dwarf beans, can be grown quite well in small beds in a town garden, but you should calculate first the quantity that can be accommodated (see page 27). You could edge your vegetable beds with dwarf box-edging. Some vegetables too can be grown in containers.

Container plants

Hanging baskets, wheelbarrows, kettles, Provencal earthenware pots, terracotta strawberry pots, even chamber pots are some examples of the endless possible containers for plants. Turn to page 60 to find out about the kinds of containers which are available today and the different types of plants which are suitable for growing in them. A season-by-season guide to caring for container plants is also given.

An example of a household item that can be adapted as a container is an ordinary glazed fireclay kitchen sink. Coat it with hypertufa. This is made of 1 part, by volume, cement, 1 part sand and 2 parts dry sifted sphagnum peat. Make sure the sink is clean and coat it with any modern bonding agent, and then apply the hypertufa, mixed with sufficient water so that it does not slide off a vertical surface, and is at least 6mm (¼in) thick. Dampness will soon give the trough a mossy appearance and clinging plants will disguise its shape.

Formal bedding

If you decide to lay out your town garden formally, there are a number of considerations to bear in mind. As with other gardens, soil, climate and rainfall will determine what can be grown, but with a town garden you might also have to contend with high walls blocking out light. This means you will have to grow plants that thrive in dark conditions and depend on greenery rather than blooms.

In limited space bare earth looks more desolate than in larger gardens, so plant tiny, quick-spreading green plants as ground cover, which will also reduce the weeds. Wallflowers and forget-me-nots associate well with spring bulbs, but they do not grow successfully in industrial cities as they dislike polluted air.

Excellent suitable summer plants for the town garden are stocks, antirrhinums, French and African marigolds, petunias, asters, alyssum, lobelia, salvias and begonias. In a mild winter lack of frost prolongs the display of the small bedding dahlias 'Coltness Gem' and 'Bishop of Llandaff'. Fuchsias are well worth growing for show and as long-lasting features, for example, 'Ballet Girl', cerise and white; 'Constance', purple with pink fringe and 'Penelope', white with pink centre.

Zonal pelargoniums (geraniums), the popular bright scarlet 'Paul Crampel' and the orange-scarlet 'Gustav Emich', will also thrive in towns. Their brash colours can be softened by including ornamental-leaved kinds, such as silver 'Caroline Schmidt' or golden 'Maréchal McMahon'. Fortunately for rose lovers town-grown roses are little affected by mildew or blackspot.

In a tiny garden points of interest can be created at different heights vertically as well as horizontally. If you want to pack the garden with plants, you should aim at having a lot of blooms at eye level rather than solely in ground level beds.

Flower bed levels Building different flower bed levels entails much hard work initially. Topsoil must first be carefully removed. Rubble or gravel is then be built up into a foundation, shaped into a miniature landscape of

Above left: *These robustly constructed wooden tubs are filled with petunias, trailing plants, lobelia and grey foliage plants, making an informal arrangement which contrasts well with the more formal surroundings.*

Above right: *A pleasing arrangement of varying shades of green is formed by foliage and flowered plants in this border.*

Left: *An urban garden embracing many different features. Crazy paving, stone slabs, different flower bed levels, well-mown grass and raised flower beds have been used to create a well-balanced small garden.*

Below left: *Clematis florida 'Sieboldii' is a striking climber. It is similar to, and makes a good substitute for, the Passion Flower in more exposed positions.*

Below right: *The popular clematis patents 'Nellie Moser' blooms in early summer and again later. It makes an attractive covering for a north or shady wall in a town garden.*

Bottom: *The Chinese Flowering Peach, Prunus persica 'Clara Meyer' which has double deep pink flowers and flourishes well in town surroundings.*

hills and valleys. The topsoil is then replaced, but as the surface area will have increased more good soil may have to be acquired. As most town topsoil is stale improve it by adding peat or fertilizer.

Once the beds are made they can be divided into small areas with brickwork or flagstone paths, which will make planting and weeding easier for you. Lilliputian terraces, like small fields or vineyards descending a hill, with hanging or trailing plants, can look very impressive.

Trees and shrubs
Trees and shrubs that thrive in town gardens are barberries, cotoneasters, Japanese laurel, box, holly, privet (the golden form if you think the green version dull) and euonymus. Suitable deciduous shrubs are the butterfly bush, *Buddleia davidii* and golden-flowered *Laburnum × watereri* 'Vossii', reaching 7–9m (25–30ft) tall. Two others are *Crataegus oxyacantha* 'Coccinca Plena' and *C. o.* 'Rosea Flore Plena'.

Magnolia × soulangeana and *M. stellata* flower freely. The prunus begin their display in February with *Prunus dulcis* (*communis*) (pale pink), followed by the purple-leaved cherry plum *P. cerasifera* 'Atropurpurea', the double peach 'Clara Meyer', and hosts of Japanese cherries, some with autumn tints. The mop-head acacia, *Robinia pseudoacacia* 'Inermis' (a smaller version of *R. pseudoacacia*) which seldom exceeds 4.5–6m (15–20ft) is also suitable.

Town garden walls
Tiny town gardens are almost always enclosed by walls, which have the advantages of shutting off noise, giving privacy and providing vertical space for climbers. As the bricks are seen at leaf fall it is important to treat them as an integral part of the garden.

Extensions to existing walls can be made comparatively cheaply with creosoted interwoven palings. Brick, though, is generally the better material. Remember, however, that any such alterations are strictly controlled by your local authority bye-laws.

Dull brick walls can be effectively enlivened by colour washing, e.g. in a pale, pretty sugar-almond colour, or white just warmed with a dash of pink or ochre.

There are a variety of attractive climbers for covering walls. These fall into two categories. Firstly, the true climbers which cling by tendrils (e.g. clematis) and secondly the twining (e.g. honeysuckle) and self-clinging climbers, which adhere to their supports by aerial roots (ivies) or sucker pads (Virginia creeper). In addition to these varieties there are wall plants which may be trained against a wall, e.g. *Chaenomeles* (*Cydonia*) – (Japanese quince or japonica), climbing roses, ceanothus and certain cotoneasters. Self-clinging climbers need no extra support, except when young. Once started they cling without aid to walls and fences. There is no need to fear the more vigorous ones, like ivy, because provided they do not interfere with drainpipes, guttering, etc., they do no

Climbing plants

Annual

Cobaea (P as A)	Maurandia	Rhodochiton
Cucurbita	(P as A)	(P as A)
Humulus (P as A)	Mina	Thunbergia
Ipomoea	Pharbitis	Tropaeolum

Tendril

Ampelopsis (D)	Lathyrus (D)	Passiflora (E)
Clematis (D & E)	Mutisia (E)	Smilax
		(D & E)
Eccremocarpus (D)	Parthenocissus	Vitis (D)
	(D)	

Twining

Actinidia (D)	Jasminum	Pueraria (D)
Akebia (SE)	(D & E)	Schisandra (D)
Araujia (E)	Kadsura (E)	Senecio (SE)
Aristolochia (D)	Lardizabala (E)	Solanum (SE)
Berberidopsis (E)	Lonicera	Sollya (E)
	(D & E)	
Billardiera (E)	Mandevilla (D)	Stauntonia (E)
Calystegia (D)	Muehlenbeckia	Trachelo-
	(D)	spermum (E)
Celastrus (D)	Periploca (D)	
Holboellia (E)	Polygonum (D)	Wistaria (D)

Walls north and east

Berberidopsis (E)	Hydrangca	Pileostegia (E)
	(D & E)	Vitis (D)
Ficus (D)	Jasminum	
	(D & E)	
Hedera (E)	Lonicera	
	(D & E)	

Shrubs, wall plants (not true climbers)

Abelia (D & E)	Cotoneaster	Indigofera (D)
Abutilon (D)	(D & E)	Itea (D & E)
Adenocarpus	Diplacus (E)	Jasminum
(D or SE)		(D & E)
	Escallonia	Kerria (D)
Buddleia (D & E)	(D & E)	Magnolia
		(D & SE)
Camellia (E)	Feijoa (E)	Phygelius (SE)
Ceanothus (D & E)	Forsythia (D)	Piptanthus (E)
Ceratostigma (D)	Fremontia (D)	Pyracantha (E)
Chaenomeles (D)	Garrya (E)	Ribes (D & E)
Colletia (D)	Hebe (E)	Rosa (D & SE)
Corokia (E)	Hypericum	Rubus (D & E)
Crinodendron (E)	(D & E)	Schisandra (D)

Key: D: Deciduous, E: Evergreen, P as A: Perennial grown as annual, SE: Semi-evergreen.

harm. In fact they could keep a wall dry and the house warm.

Adequate support can be provided by wire, preferably covered, across the face of a wall, about 5cm (2in) away from it. Wires can be effectively fixed with vine eyes, with straining bolts for tightening them, if necessary. Wall nails with lead tags are useful for individual ties for woody subjects, such as roses.

Some climbers grow easily in well-drained containers if planted in a water-retaining loam/peat/sand 'soil' mixture, described on page 67. Vigorous plants need regular feeding when fully grown.

There are a fair number of annual climbers that give quick screens. Most of them thrive better if they are planted in rich soil and fed regularly with liquid feed. Nasturtiums are exceptions as they tend not to flower so profusely if richly fed. Remember to deadhead climbing plants as this will ensure that they flower continuously.

Left: *Plastic-covered wire, stretched horizontally, vertically and diagonally between 5-8cm (2-3in) nails driven into a wall, provides an effective and cheap support for climbers.*

Above left: *Hedera helix 'Gold Heart' is an excellent, self-clinging climber which quickly covers a fence or wall.*

Above right: *Ceanothus impressus makes an excellent wall plant and grows well in full sun and well-drained soil.*

Top left: *The climber, Lonicera x americana is a strong-growing honeysuckle hybrid.*

Top right: *Parthenocissus quinquefolia, the true Virginia Creeper or American ivy.*

37

The cottage garden

The cottage garden tradition is one that is peculiarly English in character. The old-world charm of the cottager's plot owed little or nothing to any of the major developments in garden design or landscape architecture. The English cottage garden just 'happened' and its chief attraction lies in its effect of 'ordered chaos'.

The cottage garden is, to a great extent, 'natural', but nature needs a good deal of taming and direction before you can achieve an effect of studied carelessness.

The heyday of the cottage garden covered a period that roughly coincided with the Victorian era, give or take a decade or so at either end. The cottage garden had few permanent or exotic features and its hedges were the simple types bounding the neighbouring fields.

From sheer economic necessity, most cottagers had to be self-supporting in fruit and vegetables, but this did not prevent them from creating the traditional mass of colour with herbs and flowers.

Modern cottage gardens

Today the true cottagers are rapidly disappearing, being replaced by weekend countrymen and commuters. There is, however, no reason why they should not continue this beautiful traditional form of gardening, or in fact improve upon it, with the new cultivars of the older plants available today.

Upkeep of a cottage garden should

not entail as much work as a formal garden. The closeness of the plants minimizes weeding. Lawns, which are often more prominent features in contemporary cottage gardens, can be relatively small and easy to maintain in perfect condition. Plants will be renewed from seeds and cuttings by division and self-sowing – so expense of replacement can be kept low. Simplicity must always be the keynote.

The following spring and summer guide will provide the keen cottage gardener with a choice of flowers and plants which are available today.

Spring

Spring in the cottage garden can begin with the emergence of the snowdrops and winter aconites, which seed freely. The yellow buttercup-like flowers of the latter, with their attractive green ruffs, start to open during the first mild spells in late winter. Snowdrops, which come a little later, look best naturalized in grass. These are closely followed by the early daffodils and several kinds of primula.

Many specimens of primula treasured today were found surviving in old cottage gardens, although few species were known to the cottagers by their proper names. Some of these specimens are: 'Kinlough Beauty', also known as 'Irish Beauty'; 'Cottage Maid', with more restrained colouring which is similar to the latter, and several rarely cultivated lavender and pink-coloured primroses, such as 'Reine des Violettes', 'Sweet Lavender' and 'Rosy Morn'.

Even more typical, perhaps, of the cottage garden are the richly-coloured, gold-laced polyanthus. Fortunately, it is still comparatively easy to obtain seeds of these which can be sown in a cool greenhouse, in late winter, to produce full-sized flowering plants for putting out in autumn, or sown out of doors in late spring. The plants from the later sowing will be much smaller and only a proportion will produce flowers the following spring. The true

Below left: *Galanthus nivalis, the Common Snowdrop, is also called Fair Maids of February. The bulbs will thrive almost everywhere and should be left undisturbed.*

Below right: *The lovely gold-laced polyanthus which is traditionally a cottage garden flower.*

gold-laced polyanthus, or primrose is a deep mahogany-red with petals narrowly margined with gold.

Here are a few suggestions for shrubs, bulbs and herbaceous perennials that can be grown in cottage gardens in spring. Refer to the chart on page 41 for more suggestions.

Shrubs One early-flowering spring shrub that was widely grown in cottage gardens was our native mezereon, *Daphne mezereum*. It still retains its former popularity and, although sometimes short-lived, provides one of the

Below: *In the front garden of this thatched cottage the Ornamental Flowering Cherry is a magnificent sight with its branches laden with blossom. It can be grown in chalky soil, providing it is well drained.*

most welcome sights and scents of winter with its bright carmine flowers, which smell of hyacinths, that cluster the bare twigs and branches in early spring. Less often seen is the white form, *alba*.

Daphne mezereum is easily raised from seed, if you can rescue the red fruits – which, incidentally, are poisonous to humans – from the birds. It is a good idea to have a few seedling plants to act as replacements when the older plants die off.

Camellia x Williamsii 'Donation', is a vigorous growing cultivar, which flowers from winter to late spring and looks delightful in a cottage garden.

Bulbs There is a whole group of tulips that have earned the suffix 'cottage'. The cottage tulips, which are tall-stemmed with pointed petals, flower in late spring, a little in advance of the Darwins. They have, however, no more special claim to be grown on the cottage plot than any other cultivar group or species, such as the early-flowering lady tulip, *Tulipa clusiana*, the brilliant scarlet *T. fosteriana* 'Red Emperor' or the beautifully-formed water-lily tulip, *T. kaufmanniana*.

Crown Imperial (*Fritillaria imperialis*) is a spring bulb, formerly associated closely with the cottage garden, that has been elevated out of its former humble station by its present day scarcity value. Crown Imperials seem to thrive on neglect and some of the finest clumps are found in untidy corners of old gardens in places where the fork and hoe seldom penetrate.

Above: *The centre point of this cottage garden is the green sward of grass which merges smoothly into the surrounding flower beds in which roses, paeonies, hostas, 'Snow in Summer' (Cerastium tomentosam) and others create a medley of foliage and floral colour. An outstanding feature is the vigorous rambler rose, 'Albertine' which clothes the cottage wall.*

Right: *A cottage garden in which dahlias, salvias and hollyhocks provide bright colour.*

40

Cottage garden plants

Bulbs and corms—spring flowering

Allium	*Eranthis hyemalis*	Galanthus	Narcissus
Anemone	*Erythronium*	Hyacinthus	Ranunculus
Chionodoxa	*dens-canis*	*Iris danfordiae*	*Scilla sibirica*
Crocus	*Fritillaria imperialis*	*Iris histrioides*	*Scilla tubergeniana*
Cyclamen repandum	*Fritillaria meleagris*	*Muscari botryoides*	Tulipa

Bulbs and corms—summer and autumn flowering

Agapanthus	*Cyclamen*	*Galtonia candicans*	Lilium
Amaryllis	*neapolitanum*	Gladiolus	Montbretia

Annuals and biennials

Alyssum	Cheiranthus	Heliotropium	*Nicotiana affinis*
Amaranthus	Clarkia	Iberis	Nigella
Anchusa	Dianthus	*Impatiens balsamina*	*Reseda odorata*
Calendula	Godetia	*Matthiola bicornis*	Tropaeolum
Centaurea	Helianthus	*Matthiola incana*	Verbena

Herbaceous perennials

Althaea	Centaurea	Helianthus	*Paeonia lactiflora*
Anchusa	*Chrysanthemum*	Hemerocallis	Papaver
Aquilegia	*maximum*	Lathyrus	Phlox
Armeria	*Dicentra spectabilis*	*Meconopsis cambrica*	Pulmonaria
Asperula	Doronicum	Mimulus	*Pulsatilla vulgaris*
Campanula	Geum	*Monarda didyma*	*Stachys lanata*

Shrubs

Artemisia abrotanum	*Daphne mezereum*	Lonicera	*Taxus baccata*
Artemisia absinthium	Euonymus	Myrtus	*Viburnum fragrans*
Buxus sempervirens	Ilex	Rosa	*Viburnum opulus*
Chaenomeles	*Kerria japonica*	Rosmarinus	*Viburnum tinus*
Clematis	Lavandula	Sambucus	

Herbaceous perennials Many of the former cottage garden flowers have won universal esteem and we are apt to overlook their humble origins until their popular names bring them to mind. This is true of the lungwort or Jerusalem cowslip that cottagers delighted in growing under a variety of titles that included boys and girls, soldiers and sailors and spotted dog.

The above are all different names for *Pulmonaria officinalis* whose spotted leaves and pink-and-blue flowers make their appearance in spring. Today, we have the choice of several other species: *P. angustifolia* with its sky-blue flowers and narrow green leaves; *P. rubra* which, in favoured situations will open its coral blooms in late winter and *P. saccharata* which, with its white-marbled green leaves and rose-pink to blue flowers, is rather like the Jerusalem cowslip. All the lungworts make first-class ground cover and thrive equally well in sun or partial shade.

Leopards bane (*doronicum*) is another perennial. With its cheerful yellow flowers it is one of the first herbaceous plants to appear in the spring.

Summer

As spring progresses towards summer, the cottage garden provides a continuous succession of colour and fragrance. Wallflowers, often assuming their true perennial character and persisting year after year, are followed by the sweet clove-scented dianthus – the cottage pinks and clove carnations. The present-day gardener has a wide choice of the latter plants.

Pinks Interest in the old laced pinks has revived, and forms are now obtainable that flower continuously throughout the summer. 'London Poppet' is white, tinged with pink and laced with ruby-red and 'Laced Hero' has large white flowers laced with purple and a central eye of chocolate-brown.

The old garden pinks have a shorter flowering season, but give a generous display of scented blossom. 'Mrs Sinkins', a favourite white of long standing, is still among the most widely-grown of these and there is now a pink 'Mrs Sinkins' too. Other good whites include 'Iceberg' and 'White Ladies'; 'Inchmery' is a delicate shell pink of outstanding quality while 'Priory Pink' has a distinctive mauve tinge to its flowers.

The name of Allwood Brothers is practically synonymous with pinks and the modern gardener can call upon the great number of hardy hybrid pinks (*allwoodii*) for whose development and introduction Allwoods were responsible. These combine all the virtues (including fragrance) of the older

Above: *'Johann Straus', an attractive cultivar of the early spring flowering Tulipa kaufmanniana, is frequently found in cottage gardens.*

Top: *Spring in a cottage garden. Glorious colour is provided by wallflowers, violas and alpines grown on a retaining wall.*

Below: *The hedge of the semi-evergreen rose 'Albertine' forms a decorative boundary to this cottage garden. The fast-growing clematis, with its white flowers, will soon frame the whole front door.*

Bottom left and right: *The roses 'Zephinine Drounin' and 'Albertine' growing side by side, and the white rose 'Nevada'.*

forms, with great vigour and a flowering season that lasts from spring to early autumn.

In autumn the cottage garden can still be bright with Michaelmas daisies and early chrysanthemums. Nowadays, these can be supplemented with shrubs that colour attractively. The berries of shrubs such as berberis, cotoneaster and many others provide bright colour in the winter months.

Fragrant plants

It seems that almost any plant with the suffix 'sweet' has affiliations with the cottage garden. Sweet peas, sweet williams, sweet sultan and sweet rocket are just a few of the cottage flowers that have earned this name, probably because fragrance plays such an important part in determining the cottager's choice of plants. Roses, of course, were an integral part of the cottage garden.

Roses

Two of the roses which were available to the old cottage gardener, and still are to his modern counterpart, are the robust scented *Rosa gallica* 'Versicolor' ('Rosa Mundi') with light crimson flowers, heavily splashed and striped with white, and the historic R. *damascena* 'Versicolor', ('York and Lancaster') which has petals of pale pink or bluish white, sometimes mixed in the same bloom. The very beautiful, highly fragrant bourbon rose, 'Louise Odier' is another example, because with its lovely, soft pink, tinted lilac, camellia-shaped flowers, it gave the cottager joy throughout the whole of the summer.

Moss roses were another old favourite, with their intriguing aromatic, encrusted stalks and seed-pods. A cutting of the bright purplish 'Henri Martin' will grow into a vigorous 2m (6ft) tall bush. This variety is another good choice for the cottager today, as it fills the air at eventide with its exquisite perfume.

Unfortunately, the old cottage gardener did not have the good fortune to know our superb present-day hybrid tea and floribunda roses, otherwise he would have undoubtedly grown them. Today, some roses such as vigorous hybrid teas 'Uncle Walter' and 'Peace' and the free and easy floribundas, 'Masquerade' and 'China Town', will fit in admirably with the informal environment of the cottage garden, particularly if they are left almost unpruned.

The modern gardener can easily imitate or adapt some of the features of the old cottage garden. Quite often these gardens were enclosed by a hedge of the aromatic-leaved 'sweet briar' (R. *rubiginosa*) or the 'field rose' (R. *arvensis*) – either of which could have been obtained from the neighbouring hedgerows.

Climbing roses Climbing the walls of the cottage there would have been rambler roses – rose-pink 'Dorothy Perkins', white, with yellow centre,

'Albéric Barbier', the almost evergreen 'Albertine' with its fragrant blooms which looked as if they had been steeped in weak coffee, or the beautiful, loose-petalled, climbing hybrid tea 'Madame Caroline Testout'. Today these same roses could be fixed on to a rustic screen so that they hide a rubbish heap or an unsightly view.

Growing a rambler over a porch is a feature that can easily be translated to the present time. You could also create an arbour, perhaps the most characteristic feature of the old cottage garden, which was usually constructed from rustic poles and thickly engulfed in the densely-growing rambler 'Sanders' White'.

Climbers

On the walls of a cottage there is no need for formality. Climbing plants can be permitted to run riot and intertwine one with the other. This will particularly suit clematis such as *Clematis montana rubens* and many of the vigorous *x jackmanii* types. The yellow stars of *Jasminum nudiflorum* will brighten the walls in winter and in summer the more rampant and sweetly-scented *J.*

officinale, the sweet jessamine, will take over.

Other typical cottage climbers are the sweetly perfumed honeysuckles, whose garden forms are in striking contrast to our native woodbine, and *Lathyrus latifolius,* the everlasting pea which lacks the fragrance of the popular annual sweet pea, but which puts on a magnificent show each year when it flowers in late summer.

Below left: *The fragrant Sweet Pea 'Bijou', a low-growing cultivar.*

Below right: *The moss 'Henri-Martin', an old-fashioned rose that is still enjoyed today.*

Bottom: *The garden brought into contact with the house by means of the wall plants, wisteria and clematis, which flower in late spring.*

Gardens in small spaces

Many people are not fortunate enough to have even the smallest ground level garden. Despite this, however, the urge to grow something is still a strong instinct. There are ways today of satisfying this inherent desire – you can grow plants on a balcony or in a back yard, or set up window boxes and hanging baskets. This chapter tells you how to create small-scale gardens, which plants to choose and how to care for them.

Balcony gardening

Most people think of a garden as only being at ground level, but many town dwellers find that their balconies can easily be transformed into colourful areas which improve even the dreariest outlook.

Gardening on a balcony, though, demands different techniques and presents different rewards from gardening at ground level. The impact of a balcony must be immediate. The only way to ensure this is to provide masses of aggressive colour – reds and yellows for example. Colours of this nature, however, are not obtained as easily on a balcony as they are at ground level. The choice is limited because all plants must be grown in containers, none of which can be very large. Small containers mean a confined root run, a meagre supply of soil and hence a tendency to dry out quickly, causing plants to wilt or die.

The usual balcony breezes hasten the drying out process as they whistle through gaps in buildings and seldom leave flowers and plants with an opportunity for undisturbed growth.

The wind also limits the range of

plants available. When it is strongest tall growers will bend and break, trailers will become unanchored and top-heavy plants in small containers will be blown over. Except for special cases therefore, balcony plants should be low-growing, compact and sturdy.

A further problem posed by winds concerns garden debris. The balcony gardener must keep his balcony clear by collecting up fallen leaves and flower petals, and down pipes too should be kept cleared to prevent flooding after a storm. When watering plants he must also consider his neighbours, particularly those who live on the floors below.

Containers

Containers must be firmly based and square rather than tall – troughs make better containers than pots.

All containers must be secure so that there is no risk of their falling off the balcony. They should have good drainage and be raised sufficiently above the balcony floor to allow any water to escape. If this is likely to annoy others you should use drip trays.

A check must be made that the balcony will safely support the weight of the containers you wish to use as a terracotta pot, for instance, filled with moist soil can be very heavy. Make sure pots do not have sharp edges as they might in time cut through the flooring. Always spread the load to cover a wide area, placing flat pieces of wood under the feet of a tripod and broad slats under a heavy tub.

Change plants regularly to ensure contrast and vivid colour. Take out those that have passed their best and replace them with those just coming into bloom. If you do this in a closely packed trough you will damage the other plants. It is better to put the plants into individual pots which can then be put into a peat/sand mixture. This means they can be removed and replaced without difficulty. This technique has another advantage – excess moisture after watering is absorbed by the peat and sand mixture which keeps the plants moist for longer periods.

Soil for filling containers is not easily obtainable in built-up towns, but most garden shops sell potting composts, composed of loam, peat and sand with added fertilizers. If you want to sow seeds in a container it should have

Below: *This balcony has the advantage of a parapet wall, which allows climbing roses and other climbers to be grown against it. The white table and chairs and the colourful pot plants brighten the view from the kitchen on the dullest days.*

Above: *Mahonia aquifolium is a suitable shrub for shady basement areas or back yards. Its blue berries, which are coated with white bloom, are edible and make delicious jelly. Its winter coloured leaves are useful for cutting.*

Top: *A dim corner of a back yard brightened by the clever positioning of tall shrubs and softened by the gentle undulations covered in ground-hugging moss. A special feature is the virburnum, because its spreading branches soften the harsh surroundings.*

potting compost in the lower half and seed compost in the top. Nowadays it is possible to buy soil-less compost, which is composed of peat and fertilizers only. It is light in weight and retains moisture, which is an advantage on a balcony. If it is to be used in a windy spot, a 6mm ($\frac{1}{4}$in) layer of coarse sand on the surface will prevent the compost blowing away.

When a compost or good soil mixture is used, no extra feeding is needed for the first few weeks, but watering is essential. Plants grown in this fashion dry out very quickly, particularly during hot weather and watering two or even three times a day may be necessary.

Suggested plants
The following plants flourish and give lasting colour in spring and summer: marigolds (*Calendula* and *Tagetes*); Virginian stocks (*Malcolmia maritima*); campanulas; nasturtium (*Tropaeolum majus*); China aster (*Callistephus*); lobelia; nemesia; busy lizzie (*Impatiens*); wallflowers (*Cheiranthus*), petunias; forget-me-nots (*Myosotis*); pansies; arabis; periwinkle (*Vinca*); pelargoniums; London pride (*Saxifraga umbrosa*); stonecrop (*Sedum*). Also houseleeks (*Sempervivums*); crocuses, dwarf tulips, daffodils and hyacinths; antennaria; zinnias; mesembryanthemums and dwarf antirrhinums.

Even in winter the troughs and pots on a balcony need not be empty. For instance, winter-flowering heathers – *Erica carnea*; variegated ivies (*Hedera*); aucuba; dwarf conifers; skimmia;

Mahonia aquifolium, *Senecio laxifolius*, *Pernettya tasmanica* and small camellias can be successfully grown, and will brighten the view on dark, bleak days.

When space is limited, climbers can be grown up sheltered walls. Among the annual climbers there are: *Cobaea scandens*, 3m (10ft) tall, which is greenish white to violet; semi-shade-loving, vivid yellow black-eyed Susan (*Rudbeckia hirta*); morning glory (*Ipomoea*) with its brilliant shining blue trumpets and beautiful *Passiflora caerula* (passion flower). Narrow containers in more exposed positions could be filled with house leeks (*Sempervivum*) and alpine saxifrages.

Where shade prevails you can choose from:– begonias, fuchsias, ferns or trailing vines. In sunny areas petunias, salvias and geraniums can be grown in pots. In addition to decorative plants, a tub of dwarf tomatoes or a pot of green beans clambering up a wigwam of canes might be usefully included.

It is possible to buy a bag, made of heavy duty polythene, filled with compost and plant nutrients, which, when cut open can be used in a confined space to grow a variety of fruit and vegetables – tomatoes, sweet peppers, cucumbers, aubergines, strawberries and salads – as well as flowers.

Basements and back yards
If you are living in a basement flat and look out on dreary brick walls, which block glimpses of the blue sky, you can improve your view by the judicious planting of climbers and other plants in containers. The first thing to do is colour your walls with white, containing a dash of blue to simulate daylight.

If you want to use a basement or dark back yard for growing plants, you will have to choose ones that thrive in deep shade, relying mainly on the decorative effects of green foliage. Camellias, rhododendrons, hardy hybrids and *Mahonia aquifolium* might produce some flowers. Tutsan (*Hypericum androsaemum*), with small yellow flowers, *Daphnae laureola* (the spurge laurel), and *Aucuba japonica* are other possible choices. Conifers in the form of yews too can be valuable additions.

If you choose to grow the above plants in containers in your basement, remember that their roots will be restricted and they will not be able to seek their nutrients further afield. They must therefore be kept fed and receive ample water, as rain may not always reach them. In back yards these plants can be planted directly in soil. If, however, the soil is poor, it may be more sensible to use container plants instead. See page 60 for more information.

Window boxes

Window boxes are features that improve the decorative appearance of your house and give pleasure not only to you, but to your neighbours and passers-by. From inside the house they form a cheering background of flowers and leaves on grey mornings. Well-stocked and tended window boxes can make up for the lack of a garden. The shape, size and number of window boxes will be obviously dictated by the size and style of your house.

Making a window box

If you want to make your own window box measure up your window sill so that you will know how much timber you will need. Hardwoods look better unpainted and may be either oiled or varnished. Softwoods should be treated

Below left: *A beautiful arrangement of ivy, geraniums, marigolds and trailing lobelia in an old kitchen sink, which is acting as a window box.*

Below right: *An old bird cage, painted in white, hung against a wall, serving as an unusual container for trailing plants.*

Bottom left: *A basement area of a Victorian house that has been given an air of tranquility by the soft green palms, the silver-variegated ivy and an unusual floor of stone chips. The old fuel stores under the pavement have been converted into an undercover sitting-out area.*

Bottom right: *Petunia 'Sugar Plum' is an annual which is ideal as a window box plant.*

Above left: *The annual chrysanthemum cartinalum, which flowers in summer, is an attractive erect plant with colourful single flowers and stiff bright green leaves. Chrysanthemums are excellent for window boxes as they can withstand drought and draughts.*

Above right: *Planting out a window box with geraniums. These hardy herbaceous summer-flowering perennials should be well firmed in so that they are not blown over by strong winds.*

Opposite page, top: *A colourful window box in which there is a gorgeous medley of white petunias, oxeye daisies (marguerites) and deep yellow Lysimachia nummularia, which is trailing over the box, hiding its severe outline.*

Opposite page, bottom: *A summer window box filled entirely with coloured foliage plants, variegated ivies, coleus, helichrysum and others. Such an arrangement only needs the minimum of attention.*

with preservative or brightly painted. The timber should be at least 1.2cm (½in) thick and an average inside depth will be about 17–25cm (7–10in). If the window sill exceeds 127cm (5ft) in length you could make two boxes, each half the required length, to make fixing and handling easier. If the front of the box slopes at a slight angle outwards it will be easier to grow trailing plants in the box. It is best to use screws of galvanised iron or brass to hold the various sections of the box together. Drainage holes are essential and should be about 1.2cm (½in) in diameter. Make a double row of holes with about 15cm (6in) between the holes in each row.

A window box on a high sill that is not securely fixed can be dangerous, so use long hasps and staple fittings to secure the box to the window frame. The eye can be screwed to the side of the box and the hook to the window frame. This makes it easy to remove the box. Where the window ledge has a downward and outward slope use a batten of wood to level up the box.

Ready-made window boxes can be bought made of wood, galvanised iron, aluminium, plastic and fibre-glass.

Many types have galvanised containers which can be planted and then just dropped into position. This makes it easy to drop in containers with plants newly-flowering to take the place of containers in which the plants have finished flowering. This advantage can also be obtained by using the boxes for pot plants, which can be placed on shallow trays within the box.

Soil, planting and care Cover each drainage hole with a broken crock and the bottom of the box with a 2.5–5cm (1–2in) layer of crocks and gravel. Then fill the box with good soil up to about 2.5cm (1in) from the top.

Plants can either be planted directly into the soil or kept in their pots and plunged into a mixture of soil and peat in the window boxes. The latter method allows plants to be brought indoors, thus preventing them becoming frosted.

Planting in window boxes is similar to planting in the garden – hardy plants in fine weather during winter and spring, bulbs in late summer or early autumn, while semi-hardy plants should be sown in late spring.

With careful planning, a window box can be kept in flower through spring and summer. For example, you could plant bulbs first, then sweet smelling wallflowers and forget-me-nots, which will bloom after the bulbs, followed by *Nicotiana* (tobacco flower) – white for scent and lime-green for colour – then pansies and, lastly, brilliant flame and orange nasturtiums.

In order to ensure continuous flowering, remove all flower heads as they fade. In the hottest and driest period be sure to water once or perhaps twice a day (early morning and evening), because the soil dries out quickly. During the summer feed with plant food about every two weeks. Each winter clear the box out and replace the soil. It can be left empty or filled with evergreens like dwarf junipers, cypresses and ivies. Plants can be put between them the following year.

Suggested plants

Plants for window boxes must be tough so that they can withstand drought, winds and draughts. Suitable ones are: *Chrysanthemum frutescens* (marguerite or Paris daisy), double and single; gloriously coloured petunias; lobelias; verbenas and marigolds – all of which are sun-lovers; *Begonia semperflorens* and pansies, which prefer shadier conditions; fuchsias; geraniums and pelargoniums. Miniature roses, equally as tough as their larger counterparts, and hydrangeas also thrive well on balconies. During summer most bedding plants are very appropriate for window boxes.

Short, small plants are easier to keep in good trim than large plants which give an untidy appearance and should be avoided. So also should plants that grow above 60cm (2ft) tall. Brighter, gayer and more daring colour schemes are possible in window boxes, because the flowers are contained in an artifical framework, which effectively cuts them off from nature. Combinations of colour that would be unthinkable in large flower beds, become acceptable under these conditions.

Also effective are combinations of varying shades of colour, or a colour with white, e.g. yellow and orange marigolds with silvery grey foliage plants, or pink and white petunias (or pink and white geraniums) with fuchsias.

Herbs, vegetables and fruit

The herbs suitable for window boxes are low-growing ones that will thrive in pots providing they are well watered. The most appropriate ones for window boxes are *Allium schoenoprasum* (chives),

Anthriscus cerefolium (chervil), *Ocimum basilicum* (basil), *Origanum* sp (marjoram), *Petroselinum crispum* (parsley) and *Thymus* spp (thymes). The larger herbs – *Borage officinalis* (borage), *Foeniculum vulgare* (fennel) and *Salvia officinalis* (sage) also grow well, but do not reach the same height as they do in ground-level gardens.

Herbs like *Artemisia dracunculus* (tarragon), *Melissa officinalis* (lemon balm) and *Mentha* spp (various kinds of mint) have wandering roots and so thrive better in their own individual containers, otherwise they overrun their bed fellows. *Laurus nobilis* (sweet bay or bay laurel) needs rich soil.

Not only are window boxes decorative but they can also provide town-dwellers with some fresh vegetables. Lettuce, carrots and beetroot with their contrasting foliage and dwarf runner beans with their scarlet flowers look colourful. The climbing cultivars may be trained to frame the window. 'Small Fry' tomatoes have long ropes of bright scarlet fruits which are small and delicious. There are also some excellent bush tomatoes which need no supporting – for instance 'Sigmabush' or 'Histon Cropper'.

Why not try some strawberries in your window boxes? The more conventional types can be very decorative with their runners trailing over the sides. If you prefer a more compact sort, choose the delicious alpine strawberries ('Baron Solemacher' is excellent) which produce their fruits from midsummer to late autumn.

Hanging baskets

Hanging baskets are simple but attractive decorations. They should be sited where they cut out no light, where dripping water will not be a nuisance, and high enough not to obscure any view or make contact with the head of the tallest passer-by.

These baskets are made of stout galvanized or green plastic-coated wire or variously coloured polythene or alkathene in sizes ranging from 25 to 45cm (10 to 18in) across and 15 to 23cm (6–9in) deep.

Filling and planting A basket, which should be filled in late spring, should be stood in the mouth of a bucket to hold it. If the basket is a standard 30cm (12in) size, line it with about 2¼ litres (½ gallon) of damp sphagnum moss, or perforated thickish polythene, which holds the moisture better. If polythene sheeting is used several small holes

should be made at the bottom of the basket for drainage. Next fill it up to about 5cm (2in) from the rim with fairly rich compost.

A basket must not be overcrowded. A good rule is to take three plants from 13cm (5in) pots and put several smaller or trailing plants between them, and around the edge if you are filling a larger 30cm (12in) size basket.

Use plants that are just coming into flower. Place larger plants in position, angling them slightly towards the edge, firming them well in. Leave a small depression just inside the rim to conserve moisture and reduce water overflow. Seeds of nasturtiums can be pushed in at strategic positions. Then immerse the basket in water, allowing it to drain, before hanging it up.

Maintenance Avoid positions in full sun, which dries the arrangement out, and deep shade which discourages flowering. Ferns, however, thrive well in the latter situation. Water at least three times a week, even twice daily when very hot, adding a general liquid fertilizer to the water after flowering commences. Water from above or immerse the basket for a few minutes in water and drain before re-hanging. Remember to wash the leaves occasionally and dead-head regularly.

Suggested plants

The following are flowering plants for summer display: *Achimenes*; *Ageratum*; *Begonia* 'Gloire de Lorraine' and pendulous kinds such as 'Mrs Bilkey', 'Fleur de Chrysantheme', 'Golden Shower', 'Lena', 'Meteor'; *Begonia semperflorens*; calceolaria; *Campanula isophylla* and *C. isophylla* 'Alba'; *Chrysanthemum frutescens* (Paris daisy or marguerite); fuchsia, drooping cultivars such as 'Cascade', 'Golden Marinka', 'La Bianco', 'Marinka', 'Thunderbird'; heliotrope; *Lobelia erinus* and *L. tenuior*; *Lobularia maritima* (sweet alyssum); pelargonium, upright zonal kinds for top of basket, ivy-leaved sorts for draping the sides, such as 'Abel Carriere', 'Edward VII', 'Galilee', 'L'Elegance', 'Madame Crousse', 'Madame Morrier'; petunia especially 'Balcony Blended'; tropaeolum (nasturtiums), especially climbers or trailers and verbena, dwarf and trailing.

Perennials: *Aubrieta*; *Campanula portenschlagiana*; *Cerastium tomentosum*; *Cymbalaria muralis*; *Glechoma hederacea*; *Lysimachia nummularia*; *Vinca minor*.

Bulbs: (for late winter and spring display) crocus, narcissus (daffodil), galanthus (snowdrop), tulip (double).

Left: *Browallia, a greenhouse annual, makes a pretty trailer for a hanging basket in a warm sheltered spot.*

Below: *The basket should be balanced on the rim of a bucket to keep it firm while planting is done. Sphagnum moss or perforated polythene sheeting should be used as a lining before filling the basket with soil.*

Bottom right: *Small plants are knocked out of pots and planted at an angle in the centre of the basket.*

Bottom left: *A brightly-coloured hanging basket here adds charm to a period house.*

51

Patios and roof gardens

Below: *A corner of a patio enclosed by a stone wall, surmounted by trellis-work. The ornamental classical pedestal vase and the Edwardian lamp-post make excellent focal points.*

Opposite page: *This attractive patio illustrates the informal effect of house brick flooring. The surrounding trees form a wind-break and enhance the rural look.*

Patios

The patio is a comparative newcomer to British gardens, having been introduced after World War II. Its meaning, however, is different from the original Spanish one, which describes it as an 'inner court open to the sky'. Today it is an outdoor paved space that can be used for sitting out on warm days and when the lawn is soggy and the wind chilly. A patio is easily maintained and provides a hard level surface for recreation.

Siting a patio

Whether you are having a patio built or building your own, there are a number of factors, some perhaps conflicting, that you must consider.

Your reason for wanting a patio might well dictate that it should be sited near the house. If it is to be an outdoor living space then easy access from the living room is important, as is proximity to the kitchen if the patio is going to be used frequently as a dining area.

An important point to bear in mind when positioning a patio is its relation to the direction of the sun. Ideally it should have a southerly aspect, but since patios are usually used during the afternoon a westerly one might be more appropriate. If, however, because of the structure and siting of your house it is only possible to build a patio on the east side, it should be constructed so that it extends beyond the shadow cast by your dwelling. Effective wind-screening may also be necessary under such conditions.

Privacy and exposure are other aspects you should consider. There are various ways of screening a patio to give privacy as well as protection from cold winds and draughts. For the latter a screen need not be solid. Trellis wattle or interlap fencing will filter the sting out of most winds. Perhaps, however, the most attractive screens are those made in pierced concrete walling blocks in open work designs. Living screens such as hedges of box,

yew, holly or cypress can also be effective.

As the prevailing wind is south-westerly and this aspect is the sunniest, it is necessary to compromise, because a patio so sited is likely to be draughty at times. To avoid this a different position could be chosen, or the problem could be overcome by screening – either by a tall natural screen away from the patio or a lower artifical one closer to it. The former could be constructed by planting a row of tall shrubs, but as these will take some years to grow, it would be advantageous to have a temporary artifical screen nearer the patio, which can be removed when the shrubs grow taller. Tall hurdles 152–183cm (5–6ft) high make ideal temporary wind-breaks. A well-screened patio will enable you to sit out from spring to autumn.

Outlook and size

A south-facing patio may be one alternative open to you, but if the view from it is rather unpleasant and the one on the east or west side of the house is more attractive, you will have to decide whether to sacrifice sunshine or a good view.

Once you have chosen the site you can then determine how large the patio should be. As constructing a patio is a comparatively inexpensive building job, especially if you do it yourself, make it as large as is consistent with your house and garden.

Your intention regarding its use is another influence on the size of the patio. If you propose to use it as a dining area, then it need only be large enough for tables and chairs and space to move around. It needs to be much larger if it is to be used as an outdoor living area with play space for children.

The shape of your garden too will influence the size of your patio. Also if you find that your site has a steep incline the space available will be curtailed, unless you level the ground.

During summer and autumn the sun is lower and more shadow is cast, so it is

Above: *Bulbs provide bold colour on a patio in spring and early summer. They can be lifted after flowering and replaced by summer flowering plants.*

Top left: *Cascades of water flowing through a series of basins can form an unusual feature on a patio.*

Top right: *Circular stone slabs and a raised pool are the outstanding features on this patio. The container grown Fatsia japonica provides added interest.*

advisable to consider the siting and size of your patio during either of these seasons.

Patio features

A patio provides an effective link between the formality of the house and the informality of the garden. It is important, therefore, to see that the building materials used in its making are harmonious with those of the house and its architectural style.

Paving and roofs

If, for instance, you have a period cottage, mellow bricks or random stone paving of varying shapes and sizes are more appropriate than crazy paving for this style of house. The joints between the bricks should be left uncemented or, if cemented, left with numerous pockets so that if you wish you can include creeping plants that will withstand being constantly trodden underfoot.

Victorian and Edwardian cobbled and gravelled surrounds too can look attractive, but if you wish to use your patio mainly for sitting out, or as play space for children you will find that paving is more restful, drier and more suited to present-day garden furniture.

The stark line of contemporary houses call for complementary treatment. York paving looks magnificent, but is expensive and difficult to lay owing to its varying thicknesses. Cheaper synthetic stones of uniform thickness are good alternatives as they are easier to lay in sand or concrete. They are obtainable in different sizes, shapes and colours.

A mixture of coloured slabs, however, can look too fussy if you have a small patio, and in this case it is better to choose only one colour. On the other hand in the case of a large patio a uniform colour can look dull. If this is the case you could lay coloured stones, house bricks or cobbles in small areas of the patio to make it look more interesting. Alternatively you could plant flowers or small shrubs in these spaces. Before you can do this you must remove all stones, cement and concrete. Next fill the holes with a good compost to a depth of approximately 215mm (9in), and then place good soil on top.

The plants you use for this purpose should be small, otherwise their roots may lift the paving stones. Evergreens, such as heathers, are a good choice as they will not shed their leaves or develop large roots. Apart from permanent plants, colourful annuals such as phlox, nemesia and lobelia can be planted in

the spaces to brighten and give colour to the patio.

The most common type of patio roof is one made of timber joints with gaps left open to the sky – something like a pergola. It is probably best to have a covered section at one end to provide shade on very hot days. A covered section will also give you more privacy as it will restrict the view from neighbouring upstairs windows. A trellis could provide another feature. It can act as a wind-break or screen, or be purely decorative covered with climbing plants (see page 21).

Pools, barbecues and furniture

If you wish to build a small pool, either raised or sunken, in your patio area you should make a firm decision about its position before the patio is paved. Garden pools should be sited in open sun, because many aquatic plants enjoy warm water and an open site will mean a longer flowering season in the autumn and spring. Never position a pool near an overhanging tree because dead leaves create cleaning problems.

Your water supply too needs careful consideration. In most cases you will not need large quantities of water after the initial filling. You may find that the water becomes discoloured, but do not add fresh water too frequently, as in doing so you will stir up the sediment and make the water murky. If the pool can be reached with a garden hose your normal domestic water supply will be perfectly adequate.

Water-lilies are very popular pool plants and are available with yellow, white and red flowers. However, there are many other water plants from which to choose.

A number of cold-blooded fish are suitable for outdoor pools. These include goldfish, shubunkins, golden rudd, green tench and golden orfe. If you wish to keep fish in your pool, it is important to prevent the water freezing over in winter, as this cuts off oxygen from the water. A small electric heater floating on the surface will help to to prevent this happening.

Barbecues, bought or made, are becoming increasingly popular and if you propose to build a patio you could consider including one with its flue connected to one of the indoor flues, which is ideal for warming the chilly evening air. Obtain professional advice if you are intending to install electric lighting.

Your choice of furniture for the patio is important. Comfortable folding chairs should be made of synthetic fabrics and

Above: *Barbecues, which are becoming increasingly popular, can be purchased, or constructed at the same time as a patio.*

Top left: *A pool planted with water lilies and stocked with fish, which give an exciting sense of mobility. Mimulus eritea, the monkey musk and the water hawthorn, Aponogeton distachyus are other aquatic plants.*

Top right: *A decorative concrete block forms an effective screen from the wind on this patio.*

lightweight aluminium so that they will not be harmed by a summer downpour. Metal garden furniture, which will withstand the elements, is obtainable in iron and can be painted white and rendered rust-proof. Copies of Victorian cast-iron seats and tables can be obtained made from cast-aluminium and plastic. Teak and elm furniture is durable, but deteriorates after a few years if it is left out.

Patio gardening

If your patio is large enough spring and summer bedding plants can be planted in circular, rectangular or L-shaped beds. A list of bedding plants can be found on page 16. You could concentrate on a major summer display of flowering plants, or plant heathers or floribunda roses which are permanent and require only the minimum of attention. Patio plants, however, are usually mainly climbers, wall shrubs and plants in containers, as they are easy to maintain.

Use plants like clematis and honeysuckle on the walls and wind-breaks as they spread quickly and provide attractive foliage and flowers. Many climbers will flourish in tubs, but grow rather slowly, which is advantageous because a greater variety can be grown. They are best grown in beds, but be sure that

they are not a danger to damp-courses and drains, etc. For more information about climbers and container plants see pages 36 and 60.

Paving plants Crevices and pockets left between stones can be filled with creeping and prostrate plants, which will suffer little trodden underfoot. For example, cultivars of *Thymus drucei (serpyllum)* – lilac 'Annie Hill' and 'Pink Chintz'; grey-leaved *T.d. lanuginosus*; crimson *T.d.* 'Coccineus' and *Mentha requienii*. Small alpines, e.g. thrift, aubrietas and rock pinks are more tender and should be planted where they will not be trodden on.

Roof gardens

A roof garden enables you to add individuality and character to your home. It gives you the opportunity to create a different kind of garden because, as soil has to be brought in, you can use different types to grow a wider range of plants than is possible in an average garden. Another advantage is that plants grown in moveable containers allow changes to be made in the layout of the roof garden periodically.

Before embarking on an ambitious plan for a roof garden there are structural considerations that you should bear in mind. Expert advice should be obtained on the following:

Below left: *The original Spanish conception of a patio has been largely preserved here. The creepers and containers, overflowing with flowering plants, have been used to good effect. The overhanging trees, besides giving shade, create additional interest.*

Below right: *This patio has been delightfully designed. The curved flight of shallow steps, the statuary, the lead-coloured jar and the sparkling cascade descending into the pool below provide attractive features. The petunias and other plants in the raised bed, and the rhododendrons and azaleas on the periphery add colour to the scene.*

56

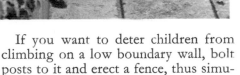

(a) Moist soil is very weighty, so is the roof structure strong enough?

(b) Is the roof surface, which will probably be of lead, bitumen, tiles or paving slabs, sufficiently thick to withstand moisture and the constant pressure exerted by the hard edges of heavy containers?

(c) Is the drainage efficient?

(d) Is roof gardening banned by local bye-laws or a landlord's agreement?

(e) Is it possible to make the boundaries safe against falling over the edge, especially if you have children?

It is worthwhile checking these points before proceeding, otherwise you could become involved in a lawsuit, or part of the building might collapse.

The size of the roof garden, which is often small and bounded by parapet walls, largely determines the layout. It is better to put soil on duckboards, which help to spread the load, rather than directly on the roof surface. Contain it outside with the parapet and inside with timber shuttering bricks or peat blocks. You will find that the latter will absorb any moisture and release it slowly to the contained soil.

If you want to deter children from climbing on a low boundary wall, bolt posts to it and erect a fence, thus simulating a ground-level garden.

Roof gardening

The problems of roof gardening are different from those of a ground-level garden. The main difference is soil depth. On the ground this is unlimited and allows the roots to seek out moisture and nutrients.

The shallow soil on a roof, however, dries out quickly and moisture can only be replaced by constant watering, as there is no underground supply from which to draw. Constant watering, however, leaches out essential plant foods, so the nutrients lost should be replaced with fertilizer. The shallow soil also prohibits the growth of thick anchoring roots, so large trees and shrubs do not usually reach maturity. Some young ones though will afford protection to low-growing vegetation.

Wind presents a special problem as it tears at the shallow-rooted taller plants and often dislodges them. A fence,

Above: *Concrete slabs in contrasting colours provide a formal paving pattern for this patio, which is screened by a wall made of concrete blocks in open design.*

Above left: *The split-bamboo screen behind the flower beds in this roof garden provides shade and protects the plants, particularly the standard fuchsias, from wind.*

Top: *In this roof garden the raised staging, which supports the flower beds, is here concealed by a cedarwood fascia.*

Below: *A niche in the wall of a roof garden can be filled in winter by bonsai, which can be bought growing in a container or alternatively, 'root wrapped'.*

Bottom left: *'Moneymaker' is a variety of tomato that can be grown in a pot.*

Bottom right: *An urban roof garden brightened with spring bulbs.*

surrounding the garden, could act as a buffer. A roof garden, however, is usually warmer than a ground-level one in winter, because heat rises from the building.

Visual aspects Roof gardening is an artificial form of gardening and it is possible to incorporate features that would be incongruous at ground level. Alternatively, you could simulate a ground-level garden by fencing in your roof garden, bordering it with medium-height shrubs and tall flowers, and laying a lawn. This will probably entail importing large quantities of soil and might mean strengthening the roof itself. It is wise therefore to consider the amount of work involved before embarking on an adventurous scheme.

Soil and watering The practical approach to finding soil for a roof garden is to obtain ordinary garden soil, which may probably be free, except perhaps for the cost of sterilizing and transporting it.

Remember that unsterilized soil contains weeds, so inspect it rigidly and remove them quickly. Heavy clay soil should be lightened by the addition of peat and coarse sand with a good handful of bonemeal to every bucketful.

Water your roof garden plants carefully, as this will minimize the loss of essential nutrients from the soil. To compensate for the loss of nutrients feed plants generously with an all

purpose balanced granular or liquid fertilizer. You will find that the close planting required to give maximum colour will make heavy demands on these plant foods.

Watering is sometimes necessary twice a day in hot weather and calls for adequate water supply. It is expensive to install a standpipe on a roof, but this can be avoided by leading a hose from a tap downstairs, through a window, to the roof.

Suitable plants and trees

One important characteristic of roof gardening is the freedom to change the layout by rearranging decorative containers. This can be done more easily if they are mounted on castors. Unattractive containers can be arranged around the periphery and hidden behind a low ornamental brick wall or fence of vertical tongued and grooved boarding.

The advantage of containers is that different types of soil may be used in each – acid for rhododendrons, azaleas, conifers, heathers, hydrangeas (which need partial shade and adequate watering), kalmia, pieris, etc – alkaline for pinks and clematis. Camellias and fuchsias are perfect container plants. As in ground-level gardens, heathers, conifers, berried and variegated shrubs can provide colour during winter. Containers can be underplanted with spring-flowering bulbs, which often come into flower earlier than those in gardens on ground-level, because of the warmth coming from the house. See page 60 for more information.

If they are given a depth of at least 35cm (14in) of soil, roses grow as well on a roof as on the ground. Climbers and bonsai are suitable for roof gardens too. See pages 37 and 32. Topiary can also look interesting in these gardens. Clipped box, privet, *Lonicera nitida* and sweet bay are easy to grow and obtainable partially shaped. Choose formal shapes, like cones or balls, rather than fantastic ones like peacocks and animals.

Vegetables and herbs

Vegetables on roof gardens will grow quickly and luxuriantly, if watered and fed lavishly. Salad vegetables grow particularly well. Vegetables and herbs should be cultivated in the same way as those on ground-level (see pages 26 and 24) or alternatively by the method described on page 46.

A sage bush or clipped sweet bay tree could be grown for both display and culinary use.

Above: *The parapet of a roof garden richly clad with an attractive, informal array of foliage and flowering plants including chrysanthemums, geraniums, helichrysum, campanulas and candytuft.*

Left: *A sophisticated roof garden which simulates the appearance of a well-planned ground-level garden. Water overflows from two concrete vessels into a round pool, forming an unusual focal point. The trees in the distance are complemented by the foliage in the raised beds.*

Container gardening

A wide diversity of design can be found in plant containers, ranging from the humble clay flower pot to the sophisticated automatically watered plant trough in polystyrene. Containers are invaluable in small gardens of all types.

Types of containers

Plastics and fibre-glass Extruded polystyrene is used for types of plant containers which have speckled or marbled finishes. They have several advantages, compared with clay or stone, as they keep the compost and plants warm, and retain moisture. Also their material is smooth and does not scratch when placed on any surface, and they are weather– and rust-proof. They are light, but fragile and need careful handling. It is better to fill and plant out the container in its permanent position. If it is likely to be necessary to move a long plastic trough after it is filled, it is better to stand it on a piece of wood.

There are numerous different shapes and sizes of plastic pots, ranging from those suitable for containing small shrubs, or a mass of bedding plants, to bulb bowls. Some plastic window boxes or plant troughs are attractively decorated by relief designs.

Fibre-glass is used to make light containers in various permanent colours which need no painting. It is a particularly valuable material because it can be made to simulate lead. Attractive lightweight containers are obtainable at reasonable prices decorated with antique designs, for example square plant containers in the style of the 1550s, King George II period tubs or early eighteenth century Queen Anne-style urns.

Wood, cement and concrete Attractive containers are available in elm, oak, teak and cedarwood. Popular dimensions start from about 60 x 30 x 30cm (24 x 12 x 12in). 'Do-it-yourself' kits are also available.

A mixture of cement and asbestos makes useful containers. While a little heavy, they are durable, frost-resistant and it is easy to drill drainage holes in them. Some are made in unusual shapes. Containers made from this material are useful as water containers for small fountains or waterfalls.

Concrete containers are often ornate. The Tudor- or Italian-style vases 50cm (20ins) high by 45cm (18in) diameter are suitable for very small areas, while Regency-style and informal fluted vases, 1m (3ft) high, look better in relatively larger areas.

Hand-made pots Beautifully designed pots in diverse shapes and sizes are increasing in popularity. Wall pots and deep containers, for trees and shrubs can be bought. One advantage of this type of container is that some potters will make pots to a customer's special design. Drainage is good if hand-made pots are well-crocked, and they can be made frost-proof if filled with good compost.

Self-watering containers The need for frequent watering of container plants can be overcome by using automatic watering containers, which are fitted with a water-filling funnel and visible water-level indicator. Water is supplied continuously by a capillary system. Alternatively there is a self-watering pot system, which usually involves a water reservoir in the double wall of the pot, with wicks in contact with the soil. The latter keep it, and in turn the roots, constantly moist.

Holders or supports The use of wrought-iron stands, etc. for garden display is becoming increasingly popular. These pedestals have a plant container or a platform top for alternative displays. In some designs the height is adjustable; others are made for automatically-watered containers; and there are wall supports for some troughs. Sometimes the design is in scrollwork, which is covered in white plastic. This makes it attractive and weather-proof. A fibre-glass tub with a wrought-iron tripod could be another possible useful purchase.

Below: *A modern pre-cast concrete container filled with tulips and polyanthus.*

Opposite, top: *The different sizes, shapes, colours and materials of the containers give character to this paved area.*

Opposite, bottom left: *Terracotta clay pots are available in a wide variety of decorative designs.*

Opposite, bottom right: *Plant containers made of wood, concrete, fibre-glass and clay.*

Inventive ideas

There is no need to spend lavishly on ornamental vases for the garden because with a little ingenuity you will be able to find a variety of containers. Below are a few suggestions.

(a) Old wine barrels, obtained from wine merchants, can be sawn in half and drilled at the bottom. They should be treated with a wood preservative.

(b) Old chimney pots, plain and decorated, obtainable from builders' yards, can be given a concrete base, with drainage holes made by inserting wooden plugs before the concrete has set. The plugs can be knocked out afterwards.

(c) Domestic water tanks of various sizes and shapes. Holes should be drilled in the base.

(d) Old wash coppers, which are often about 1m (3ft) in diameter, make excellent containers. Their rounded bottoms can be flattened by beating out so that they stand more stably. On exposure to weather they acquire a pleasing patina. Cast-iron coppers are not so desirable, because they are difficult to drill for drainage.

(e) Split-cane new potato baskets, obtainable from greengrocers in spring, make useful plant containers for one or two seasons.

(f) Farm sales are sometimes fruitful with, say, cheap feeding troughs, which are acceptable in gardens if they are painted. Disused hay-racks fixed to a wall make unusual garden features. They should be lined with fine mesh wire netting, or perforated polythene, and then filled with soil.

(g) An excellent find is an old wooden wheelbarrow which, drilled at the bottom and filled with compost, makes an excellent moveable container for plants. The wood can either be left in its natural state and treated with transparent preservative, or gaily painted.

(h) Large earthenware rhubarb forcing

pots, turned upside down, make lovely pots for plants. There is a hole at the top, which becomes a drainage hole when the pot is inverted.

With a good imagination you will find there is no limit to the possibilities. In towns old baths, hip baths and old-fashioned laundry baskets have been marshalled for growing plants, while in the country plants are often seen enlivening hollowed-out old tree stumps.

Container plants

Many plants will grow in containers, providing they are given one the right size and the correct soil. See page 67 for a list of flowering plants.

Trees and shrubs

Some trees and shrubs are specially suitable for planting in containers. If they grow too large they must be replaced, but with their roots confined many adapt themselves to the conditions and grow comparatively small.

Some of the exquisite Japanese maples, *Acer palmatum*, are particularly suitable for containers, because they are slow-growing and tend to be dwarf.

The spotted laurel, *Aucuba japonica*, with its gold-spotted leaves and red berries is very suitable. With its striking glossy palmate leaves, cream flowers and black berries, there is nothing more dramatic than *Fatsia japonica* which is tough and will withstand dryness for short periods, or exposure to the wind and sun.

Camellias particularly make marvellous early-flowering container plants, with their bright magnificently coloured and shaped blooms. Although appearing delicate, they thrive well in most weather conditions. Camellias should be grown in rich acid to neutral soil, their roots should be kept moist and their leaves sprayed on hot days. Hydrangeas, with their great mop-headed colourful flowers, are also suitable as container plants as long as their roots are never allowed to become dry. They should be placed in semi-shade and watered lavishly.

Evergreens

Deciduous trees and shrubs become bare in winter, so evergreens are more suitable in containers.

Conifers are particularly effective, being dwarf and slow-growing and architectural in outline—either conical, columnar, globular or prostrate. Being wind resistant they are liable to be blown over, so put them in heavy

Opposite page: *This concrete base, surmounted by an old brightly-painted pump is a novel idea for a container garden. The gay, tightly-packed pansies complement it beautifully.*

Left: *A brightly painted old wooden wheelbarrow makes an attractive container. This one is planted up with hyacinths and muscari.*

Centre left: *Camellia ×　williamsii is one of many camellias which brighten up dark winter days.*

Bottom: *Hydrangeas make superb pot plants if kept well watered. H. macrophylla 'Blue Wave', shown here, is one of the best blues.*

Below right: *The panniers carried by this old statue make unusual containers. They are filled here with variously coloured ivies, bringing colour to a dark corner.*

Above: *A group of architectural contemporary containers suitable for an expansive paved area. They are filled here with a range of colourful spring plants.*

Right: *An old glazed butter crock acts here as a container for spring daffodils.*

Opposite top: *A visit to a well-run nursery often provides inspiration. Here, thrift, primroses, variegated ivies and rock phlox await purchasers.*

Opposite centre: *Rhododendron williamsianum is a rounded compact bush, which has coin-shaped bronze leaves and shell-pink flowers in spring. It is a hardy shrub and grows to about 150 cm (5ft) high.*

Opposite bottom: *Colourful annuals can be raised from seed in spring, without using a greenhouse, by sowing in a box which has been placed in a polythene bag. The latter should be inflated and closed tightly with a rubber band.*

broad-based tubs. A good layer of drainage pebbles helps to stabilize them. Because they shed their foliage gradually, they do not signal ill-health or dryness immediately. For this reason it is important to keep young plants well-watered. Give their foliage a thorough spray with clean water when the weather is hot. Adding peat to their soil helps retain moisture and renders the soil slightly acid, which the majority of conifers prefer.

Bulb flowers and climbers
Bulb flowers suitable for growing in containers include all the normal spring flowering kinds, such as hyacinths, narcissi and tulips. Choose sorts which do not grow too tall, otherwise strong winds will damage them. Beautifully coloured, summer-flowering, scented lilies are very successful in pots, but they must be staked.

Among the annual climbers suitable for growing in containers is the blue morning glory (*Ipomoea*). The purple *Cobaea scandens* which is usually treated as an annual, will grow successfully too, if given a warm position. Hardwood climbers are also very successful and effective if kept well-watered. Growing in a restricted space, vigorous ones will not grow to their full extent. Suitable climbers for pot culture are Virginia creeper, gold- and ivory-splashed ivies, honeysuckles, *Euonymous fortunei* (for low supports) and roses.

Care of container plants

As container plants thrive in different conditions from other plants, a season-by-season guide to caring for them is given here.

Winter

Winter is a period for repair, renovation and renewal. All areas should be kept swept clean of dead leaves, etc., because they harbour pests and disease spores. A check must be made that the drainage holes of containers are not choked with rubbish or fine soil washed in them by summer rain. Excess water from winter snow, frosts and rain is likely to freeze if it cannot flow away freely. The roots are then likely to be starved of water and the plants might die or the container become cracked.

It is also important to see that water drains quickly from the floor on which the pots are standing, because plants and containers can be seriously damaged by contact with too much water. It is important, therefore, to see that all containers are standing off the floor.

Make sure too that the supports of climbers, straining wires or trellis-work, are securely fixed to walls and also that last year's dead growth is removed, because its weightiness might cause damage if blown down by high winds.

One of the principal aims of a container gardener during the winter should be to protect the plants against frost by keeping the surroundings slightly above freezing. This can, of course, be done by installing soil warming or under floor heating, etc. Such devices, however, use a lot of electricity, and are expensive to install.

To keep plants as warm as possible place containers in sheltered positions and protect with sacking or straw, but make sure that rain is accessible to the plants, otherwise they will dry out. A light soil mixture helps drainage and prevents soil freezing. Scraping away the top 5 cm (2 in) of soil and replacing it with peat also helps to keep the soil warmer. If a root ball becomes frozen let it thaw out naturally in a sheltered place, or take it to a shed or cold greenhouse, if you have one.

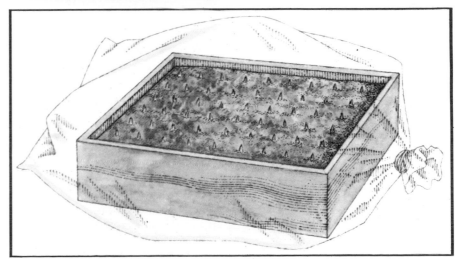

Winter is the season during which you should renew your plants and plant up new containers. If your containers are over 30cm (1ft) deep, permanent plants can be underplanted with spring bulbs. Because of their lightness and water-retaining property, soil-less composts are useful for container gardening, but they have the disadvantage of blowing about in the summer breezes. This can be overcome by incorporating some heavier soil with them or top-dressing with about 2.5cm (1in) of shingle or limestone clippings.

Spring

Plants in containers, because they are a little warmer, are usually a little more advanced than those in the open ground. All danger of frost will not have passed by spring, however, so do not be tempted to put out tender plants.

Colourful annuals and other plants for window boxes and troughs can be raised from seed. It is not necessary to have a greenhouse for this purpose as many seeds will germinate in your house. They should be sown in pots or boxes and then placed in a polythene bag. The latter should be inflated and closed tightly with a rubber band. The warmth and humidity will soon cause germination. Examine it daily for condensation. If high, remove the seed container, turn the bag inside out and put it back. Keep the seeds in a warm place such as the airing cupboard at first. Put them on a window sill later to give them good light but less warmth. Harden them off by putting them outdoors on a warm day when the seedlings are larger.

Many seeds can be sown directly in containers in early spring. If this is done, growth should be hastened by covering them with a sheet of glass weighed down with a stone, which will prevent it being blown off by the wind. Cuttings incidentally can be rooted similarly. It is better, however, to plant some containers out permanently with dwarf shrubs, conifers and rock plants to give instant results. Remaining containers can be filled with annuals raised from seed in late spring.

It is important to clear out spring bulbs as soon as the flowers fade so that they do not look untidy when they die down in their containers. Put them in a box of peat or soil, or in a garden.

You should water newly-sown seeds and plants constantly from early spring. You may find that with a comparatively dry compost, the first good watering drains away quickly leaving the roots relatively dry, so the first thorough watering should be followed by another. As growth becomes evident feed with a liquid or granular fertilizer. At first use less than the recommended dose. Make sure that the soil is thoroughly wet before feeding.

Your aim in spring should be to have all the preparation and planting complete to ensure colourful containers later and to have all wall surfaces prepared to house the climbers that are busily producing new growth.

Summer

The pleasures of patio, roof gardens and balconies can be fully enjoyed during the summer. Seeds of annuals can be sown in pots to give vivid colour later in the season, e.g. alyssum, candytuft, nigellas, mignonette, virginian stocks, pansies, arabis and others.

Low-growing plants can be planted at the base of trees, shrubs and taller plants already in containers. During warm summer days and evenings container plants are at their best. Boxes of flowers in bloom can be bought from garden centres and planted out to give an instant blaze of colour. To help you choose, here is a selection of flowering plants.

White: alyssum, begonia, daisy, candytuft, dianthus, echium, eschscholzia, forget-me-not, gazania, linaria, lobelia, pansy, petunia, *Phlox drummondii,* polyanthus and verbena.

Yellow: eschscholzia, gazania, limnanthes, nasturtium, nemesia, pansy, polyanthus, *Tagetes signata* and wallflower.

Red: anagallis, begonia, *Dianthus sinensis,* nasturtium, nemesia, petunia, *Phlox drummondii,* polyanthus and portulaca *Silene pendula,* verbena and wallflower.

Blue: anagallis, anchusa, forget-me-not, lobelia, nemesia, nemophila, pansy, petunia, phacelia, polyanthus, verbena and viscaria.

Choose plants that have moist roots, which are disease and insect free, and ones that have small buds, rather than flowers, (as this tends to mean that the plants are starved or sown too early). Keep them in the cool until you can plant them. Prepare your containers using a mixture of 7 parts by volume loam, 3 parts peat and 2 parts dry coarse sand with a little added fertilizer, or a proprietary no-soil mixture. The containers should be as large as possible so that they can hold a considerable quantity of soil, which retains moisture. An extra addition of peat will enhance this property.

Water the boxes before planting and lift each plant out with a good ball. Plant with a trowel, spreading the roots and firm in. Water again and shade the newly-planted container for two days. When they are growing well look out for disease daily, dead-head to ensure continuity of blooming and replace any plant that dies.

All container plants must have water always available at their roots. This ensures that they can draw up vital moisture lost by transpiration and absorb the nutrients in the water. Watering twice a day is not too lavish during hot weather. To minimize loss by evaporation, it is helpful if the plants can be given shade for some time each day.

When watering, the soil must become completely soaked. Water should issue freely through the drainage holes. Watering must be done gently and repeatedly, if necessary until the soil is thoroughly wet.

Transpiration is slowed if the foliage is thoroughly wet, so the plant must be drenched. A humid atmosphere can be created by flooding the floor. If you do this on a balcony make sure that it will not be a nuisance to the neighbours. Watering is best done in the early morning or late afternoon, so that the

Below: *This ornate and traditional pedestal container is suitable for a town or cottage garden.*

Below left: *Roses, hydrangeas and geraniums all flourishing in clay pots. As they dry out quickly they need constant watering.*

Below right: *Old, deep, painted wooden tubs make ideal containers for hydrangeas.*

Right: *Cobaea scandens, from South America, is a gorgeous half-hardy climber with white or violet trumpet-like blooms and fresh green leaves. It grows best on a wall in a sheltered, warm position.*

Below left: *A magnificent pedestal vase of classical design filled with geraniums, which will make an ideal focal point in a paved town garden.*

Below right: *The prostrate form of Juniperus sabina is a suitable subject for a container. Its soft greyish-green foliage emits a distinctive aromatic smell.*

loss by evaporation is at a minimum and the plants have some hours to absorb the water. Sprinkler systems are not very suitable for containers in small spaces, because they are not sufficiently concentrated and can be a nuisance to your neighbours. Sometimes, however, it is possible to work such equipment at low level and water various areas for an hour at a time.

Drainage holes should always be kept clear, not only to ensure a good flow of water, but also to draw air through from the atmosphere.

Autumn

During this season the container gardener should make the most of evergreens, and the few shrubs and trees that will survive the snow and frost. Evergreens can have gold, silver, grey and blue, as well as green, foliage.

Dwarf and slow-growing conifers are particularly valuable in this season, not only for their colour, but also for their shapes which look delightful silhouetted against mist or snow. The tiniest are excellent for window boxes. *Juniperus communis* 'Compressa' is a blue-green pillar, only 60cm (2ft) tall; spreading *J. procumbens* 'Nana' is no more than a few centimetres (inches) high; *Chamaecyparis lawsoniana* 'Minima Aurea' is cone-shaped with elegant twisted golden foliage; cushion-shaped *C. obtusa* 'Pygmaea' has fanning foliage, turning red at the tips in winter; and *C. thyoides* 'Andelyensis' turns almost plum-coloured.

If you plant heathers or ericas, their existing flowers will persist during snowy weather, though new flowers will not open until after the thaw. In some areas with hard winter *E. Carnea* does not bloom until spring and true heather (*Calluna*) will never bloom in winter. Heathers should be planted in acid soil, although *Erica carnea* cultivars will tolerate a little lime. Some cultivars have brilliantly coloured foliage – rich tints of gold and red that make them look as colourful as flowers. They mix effectively with dwarf conifers and grow well in tubs.

During autumn plant camellias or rhododendrons which will last into winter. The former are hardy, have beautiful leaves and some sorts flower in early winter – *Camellia japonica* 'Nobilissima' and *C. x williamsii* for example. Newly planted camellias should be protected from frost with peat around their base. Do not plant them exposed to early morning sun, because rapid thaw can damage the flowers after a frost.

A large tub will take a rhododendron, which should be planted in acid soil. One cultivar, 'Lee's Scarlet' will bloom at Christmas – others following quickly, *Rhododendron mucronulatum* and *R.* 'Praecox' for instance. There are many species and cultivars of rhododendron which bloom in succession from late autumn to the following late summer.

In autumn early-flowering bulbs should be planted – snowdrops, crocus species and aconites will be the first to bloom, followed later by narcissi and tulips. They can be underplanted in containers of heathers and conifers and will enhance their foliage colours. Many bulbs may be grown in boxes, so you can keep replacing those that have passed their best, providing a constant succession of bright colour.

In the autumn you should look ahead and prepare your containers for colder weather. Clean up all the containers in use. Lift, divide and replant perennials where necessary. A few plants prefer to be moved when the soil is warmer, so leave these till spring. They include delphiniums, michaelmas daisies, kniphofias, scabious and pyrethrums.

When all cleaning up has been completed mulch all plants in containers with peat or some of the leaves that have been falling from the trees, in the last few weeks. If this mulch is likely to be dislodged by winds, anchor it with a layer of pebbles or a piece of chicken wire cut to shape.

Below: *Plants in containers on the patio need some attention before the winter weather sets in. Replace the soil, washed away by the rain and watering, with top dressing.*

69

Index

Pictures supplied by

A. de Rahm : 9(b)
Amateur Gardening : 20(br)
Barnabys : 30(l)
Bavaria Verlag : 28(b)
John Blair Rose Garden, Courtesy Colonial
Williamsburg : Contents
Michael Boys : 24(l)
Heidede Carstensen/Jacques Hartz : 62
Casa Pupo : 44(r)
Cement & Concrete Association : 62(t)
R. J. Corbin : 14(tr)(br) 19(t) 23(tl)(tr) 24(tr)(br)
Bruce Coleman : 41(b)
26(tl) 27(b) 28(t) 31(t) 33(bl) 37(b) 44(l) 48(r)
51(tr)(br) 54(tl) 57(b) 67(bl) 69
J. Downward : 34(t)
Alan Duns : 37(cl)
Richard Einzig : 47(bl)
V. Finnis : 6 10 11(r) 14(l) 17(br) 19(b) 25(t)
26(tr) 29(tr) 37(tl) 40(t) 49(b) 50 58(bl) 66(b)
P. Genereux : 27(t) 51(tl)
I. Hardwick : 39 42(t) 63(t)
Nelson Hargraves : 55
J. Hovell : 60
P. Hunt : 18(tr) 37(tr) 64(b)
G. Hyde : 17(tl) 20(t) 21(b) 24(cb) 36(tr)
L. Johns : 23(b) 25(b) 52 58(t) 59(t)
Paul Kemble : 57(tl)(tr) 59(b)
R. Kaye : 18(tl)(br)
Sam Lambert : 46(t)
John Ledger : Introduction
J. Markham : 38(l)
E. Megson : 12 61(t)
M. Newton : 63(bl)
Paf International : 56(bl)
R. Perry : 32(b)
Pictor : 53
R. Proctor : 32(t)
R. Rutter : 8(t) 30/1 33(tr)(tl) 34(b) 61 63(br)
65(t) 66(t) 67(t)(br) 68(bl)
M. Slingsby : 63(cl)
D. Smith : 33(br) 47(tr)
H. Smith : 11(l) 15(b) 16 17(tr) 18(bl) 20(br)
21(t) 22(bl) 26(bl) 29(bl) 31(b) 35 36(tl)(b)
40(b) 41(t) 42(bl)(br) 43 46(b) 47(br) 48(l)
49(t) 42(bl)(br) 43 46(b) 47(br) 48(l) 49(t)
51(bl) 54(tr) 55(tl) 56(br) 65(c) 68(t)(br)
Sutton Seeds : 15(t)
Syndication International : 7(b)
Colin Watmough : 37(cr)
Elizabeth Whiting : 45